Bedtime Stories for Kids

Mindfulness Meditation Stories About Unicorns, Mermaids, Dragons, Dinosaurs, and Aliens to Help Your Children Relax and Fall Asleep Fast

© Copyright 2020 - All rights reserved.

The content within this book may not be reproduced, duplicated or transmitted without direct written permission from the author or the publisher.

Under no circumstances will any blame or legal responsibility be held against the publisher, or author, for any damages, reparation, or monetary loss due to the information within this book, either directly or indirectly.

Legal Notice:

This book is copyright protected. It is only for personal use. You cannot amend, distribute, sell, use, quote or paraphrase any part, or the content within this book, without the consent of the author or publisher.

Disclaimer Notice:

Please note the information within this document is for educational and entertainment purposes only. All effort has been executed to present accurate, up to date, reliable, complete information. No warranties of any kind are declared or implied. Readers acknowledge that the author is not engaging in the rendering of legal, financial, medical or professional advice. The content within this book has been derived from various sources. Please consult a licensed professional before attempting any techniques outlined in this book.

By reading this document, the reader agrees that under no circumstances is the author responsible for any losses, direct or indirect, that are incurred as a result of the use of information within this document, including, but not limited to, errors, omissions, or inaccuracies.

Contents

INTRODUCTION 1
    HOW TO USE THIS BOOK.. 2
CHAPTER 1: THE STORIES OF DOPEY THE DREAMY DRAGON 4
    DOPEY THE DREAMY DRAGON BECOMES DOPEY THE DARING DRAGON 5
DOPEY FOLLOWS HIS DREAM 8
    DOPEY THE DREAMY DRAGON MARCHES ON... 11
    THE DREAMY DRAGON MASTERS HIS NIGHTMARE 14
DOPEY THE DREAMY DRAGON LEARNS TO CONTROL HIS FIRE 17
CHAPTER 2: UNA THE ULTRA-SONIC UNICORN YARNS 21
    HOW UNA THE UNICORN FOUND FRIENDS.. 22
    UNA AND JEREMY SAVE THE LITTLE UNICORN 25
    UNA THE UNICORN STOPS SHOWING OFF 28
    UNA AND THE PATCHWORK QUILT 32
    UNA THE UNICORN FINDS PEACE... 35
CHAPTER 3: THE WATERY WORLD OF THE MYSTICAL MERMAIDS . 39
    HOW MERCI CONQUERED HER FEAR 40
    THE MISCHIEVOUS MERMAID LEARNS TO BE KIND................................... 43
    MERRY LEARNS TO CONTROL HER TEMPER 46
    MICHELLE SHARES HER TREASURES 50

I AM HAPPY TO BE ME..53
CHAPTER 4: THE TALES OF DOUGHNUT, THE DANCING DINOSAUR
....57
    DOUGHNUT DRESSES UP..58
    DOUGHNUT, THE DINOSAUR, GOES TO SCHOOL................................60
    DOUGHNUT VISITS HIS GRANDMOTHER..64
    DOUGHNUT GOES TO THE SEASIDE..67
    DOUGHNUT, THE DANCING DINOSAUR, MAKES MUSIC........................71
CHAPTER 5: THE ADVENTURES OF ABBLESOC, THE AWESOME ALIEN 75
    ABBLESOC THE ALIEN FINDS A HOME..76
    ABBLESOC THE ALIEN FACES THE BULLIES..78
    ABBLESOC MEETS DR. BOB..86

Introduction

Do you sometimes shudder when you see what your children are watching on TV? Do you like the gratuitous violence that seems to be a large part of so many "children's" comics and video games?

Young children live in the fantasy world they are offered. We should offer something better. These stories are about being human; decent humans.

What these stories are NOT about:
- Being violent
- Being aggressive
- Winning at all cost
- About hurting others
- Intolerance – for other creatures and other ideas
- About casual cruelty
- There are no guns, no bombs, no knives, no cowardly use of weapons.

These are mindful stories. They are carefully designed to let your child know their own power and their unique inheritance - with an acceptance of the wonderful variety of experiences and lives we have all around us.

You will find descriptions using all our senses. Color, scent, sound, movement, and touch are how we experience life, yet we are often unaware of ourselves. The world moves on, and we get left behind!

The little creatures in this book each have their own stories. They face challenges, just as we do. The tales tell how they overcome them and learn of themselves, their weaknesses, and their strengths.

Just like us, they face prejudice, pride, anger, greed, and selfishness. But when they come face to face with themselves, they learn to accept what they are and to take pride in it. These creatures may all appear to be different – but they have the same grown-up problems that our children face.

Your child can follow the adventures of Abblesoc the Alien as she learns that being different is fine. You can follow Dopey the Dreamy Dragon as he learns to grow up. The Mermaids in their Watery World also face challenges -just like us all – how do they deal with them?

And then there is Una the Ultra-Sonic Unicorn, and if you don't know what ultra-sonic means – it doesn't matter, but your child will know! Finally, we have Doughnut, the Dancing Dinosaur, who dances his way through life in his own generous, childlike manner.

When you read these little stories to your child, you will find they have a relaxing part at the end. Read with care and patience; they will help send your child to sleep – not with nightmares, but with a calm acceptance of who they are. It's all about being human.

You and your child might even have your own favorite character, as I do. Can you guess which is mine?

How to Use this Book

Here are suggestions for ways you can use this book of stories. They help your child relax and make it easier for them to fall asleep naturally.

The stories are divided into five chapters, with each chapter having five stories. Most stories can be read in any order, but the first of each chapter sets the scene for the dragon, the unicorn, and the alien, and you may like to read that one first. The dragon stories are best read in order.

Children like repetition; it gives them some control and a feeling of security. The mermaid stories have the same introduction to each story. You may find that your child will help you read the first part after having had it read to them twice. You may even "forget" a character's name - like the Mermaid's - from time to time, giving your child a chance to correct you, and making it more fun for your little one.

Towards the end of each story is a time for relaxation. It is so easy to rush this part, but we become aware of all our senses with mindfulness. We see almost instantaneously; *hearing* takes a fraction longer. Still, to organize our sense of touch and to feel takes longer. We need to take the time to adjust our muscles, to listen, and then adjust the rhythm of our breathing. And as we breathe more slowly, we both mentally and physically relax.

You will notice a lot of ellipses (...) towards the end of each story. It is a suggestion to pause. Give your child a chance to catch up...

If you are very observant, you might adjust your reading pace to your child's breathing. If you can do this, you will find a great sense of empathy with your child. And if you then feel relaxed, so will your child.

These little tales will lower your child's energy levels and help them go to sleep in a relaxed and comfortable frame of mind. Reading or telling stories to a child at bedtime has a long history of building successful and lasting family relationships.

The best advice is simply to enjoy the stories. For a short time, enter into their world and relish the small window of time you have to relax with your very special children.

Chapter 1: The Stories of Dopey the Dreamy Dragon

Dopey the Dreamy Dragon becomes Dopey the Daring Dragon

Dopey was afraid. He was a very little, very fragile dragon, and he was all alone. He'd gone out to play in the sunshine with his sisters - but now he was lost. He had nowhere to go, and his little heart trembled. He was very sad; he was very thirsty; he just wanted someone to love him.

The sun was going down, and the shadows were lengthening. Dopey crept into a woodshed and tried to sleep - a tiny, shivering ball among the logs.

Suddenly he heard a child's voice and pricked up his ears. He tried to vanish among the logs, but he was too big. He waited as the voice came closer - and closer. Dopey gave a sad, tiny cry - it was the bravest thing he had ever done.

The voice belonged to Jenny. Jenny was six years old and afraid to go to school. She was afraid the other children would laugh at her; she was afraid she would not be able to do arithmetic or would get into trouble. But most of all, Jenny was afraid to leave her mother. What if something happened while she was away?

But Jenny felt lonely too. There was no one to play with at home, no one to giggle with, no one to share jokes and games with.

When she saw the little lost dragon, her heart melted. She went quiet and still. Dopey went quiet and still. They watched each other - the red-eyed dragon and blue-eyed girl. Jenny slowly reached out a hand, slowly she touched his spiny back, and very gently, she stroked him. And the little dragon started to sigh contentedly- softly because he was a very small dragon.

But when Jenny tried to pick him up, his little spikes stood on end, and he backed even further into the woodpile.

So, Jenny went to tell her mother about the dragon in the woodshed.

"He may be thirsty," her mother said. "Offer him some water, and he might come to you."

Jenny went back to the woodshed. Dopey was still there. When he saw the water, he very bravely moved forward to suck it up - it tasted so good! Feeling comfortably full, he let Jenny pick him up gently and carry him to the house. The kitchen was nice and warm. Jenny's mom had put a soft towel into a shoe-box, and Dopey settled himself there by the stove. Before long, he was fast asleep.

Very soon, Dopey grew a little bigger - but he refused to go anywhere without Jenny. He followed her to the bathroom. He sat on her in bed. He gazed at her when she ate, and he was under her feet the whole time (unless he was asleep). Jenny loved him very much - but sometimes he just got in the way! He woke up early and jumped on her face long before the sun shone into her room. He wanted to play all day and most of the night - it was exhausting!

"Maybe he gets a little bit bored?" questioned Jenny's mom. "Wouldn't it be nice if he'd just go outside and play sometimes?" But every time they put him outside, he stayed close to the door - too frightened to explore the garden; he might get lost again!

"He's too afraid he'll get lost and won't be able to get back in," said Jenny.

"Perhaps if he had a little cat flap door, he would know we were always there for him, and he wouldn't be so timid," said her mom. Remember, Dopey was still a very small dragon.

So, the cat flap was fixed and shown to Dopey. It took him a little while to understand it. He put his head through and backed out. Next time, Jenny gave him a gentle shove - and he found himself in the garden - and the door was closed. Dopey sat down and thought. He examined the door and found the cat flap. He pushed - and it moved - he pushed harder - and it opened - he shot inside - spikes on end, but secretly rather pleased - what a clever little dragon!

Soon, Dopey was spending more and more time out in the garden. He felt safe. He knew he could return whenever he wanted to. He had never felt so happy. Dopey played with the grass, he chased the butterflies, he pounced on fluttering leaves - and he spent a whole day guarding a smooth, round stone.

He even practiced making fire come out of his mouth - though he wasn't very good at this yet.

Jenny felt a little bit jealous - Dopey as having such a good time outside doing his own dragon thing. And although Dopey still loved her, came to jump on her, and lick her face during the night, he no longer seemed afraid to leave her. In fact, now, Dopey was the "Daring Dragon!"

But Jenny was bored. Her mom was always busy, and Jenny felt she wanted a friend - someone her own age to chat with, someone to share her music with, someone to make bad jokes with. But she was afraid to leave her mom. What if her mom suddenly needed her?

"Well, I can't make you a cat flap," said her mom. "But I can make sure you know I am here - and safe. I am going to talk with your teacher."

Mrs. Jones, Jenny's teacher, listened carefully. She made a plan.

"There is Edward," she said. "He's new here and needs a friend. I can ask his mom if he could go to tea with you and Jenny. And, of course, if Jenny gets frightened at school, I will call you, and you can speak to her."

Edward came to tea the very next day. He wanted to play in the garden, so they went outside, leaving the two moms to chat in the kitchen. Edward thought Dopey was the finest dragon he had ever seen. (He hadn't actually seen a real dragon before.)

The next morning, when Edward rang the doorbell on his way to school, Jenny was ready - although a little bit nervous. But she didn't want him to think she was frightened!

The two walked to school with their moms. At the gate, Edward grabbed hold of Jenny's hand and ran inside the schoolyard.

Jenny's mom waited all day for the phone to ring; it never did. When she went to collect her at the school gate, Jenny came running out, a happy smiling face, yelling goodbye to her new friends.

"I'm as daring as Dopey!" she cried gleefully.

Dopey Follows His Dream

Dopey was growing. He was getting bigger and bigger. He was far too big to go through the cat flap. And he was getting lonely.

Jenny was at school all day, and mummy was busy working in the house. It was time he moved on – but where?

Now, Dopey had the most splendid dreams. But one dream kept coming back again and again. He would wake up in the garden or in the room where he went to bed each night – and remember his special dream.

He dreamed – in bright colors – that he was in a far-off land where there were lots and lots of other dragons. Dopey had only seen real dragons when he was very tiny. But the dream dragons seemed to be asking him to come and find them. They were asking him to come and play. But when he woke up, he would find he was all by himself. He longed to join those dream dragons.

One morning, he woke from his dream and decided he WOULD go and find the dragons. He had woken up just as he was following a path in his dream, up a high mountain, to Dragon Land.

Dopey packed a small bag with some peanut biscuits and a bottle of water. Then he set put into finding Dragon Land.

But which way should he go?

Beside the garden, the gate lived a green toad.

" Mr. Toad," asked Dopey, "do you know the way to Dragon Land?"

"No," said Mr. Toad, "but if you go up towards the mountain, you will find the way."

So Dopey continued towards the mountain. Soon he came across some cows in the field.

"Hello, cows," said Dopey. "Do you know the way to Dragon Land?"

"No," said the cows, "but if you go up towards the mountain, you will find the way."

So Dopey continued across the fields towards the mountain. He was feeling thirsty by now, so he drank his water, carrying the empty bottle with him.

Soon the fields rose, and the mountain was very close - and it looked very steep. Dopey was getting tired - but he went on, more slowly now.

An eagle, high in the sky, looked down at Dopey. "That little dragon looks lost," the eagle thought. He flew down to have a closer look.

"Are you lost, little dragon?" he asked.

"I'm looking for Dragon Land," replied Dopey. "Do you know the way?"

"Yes," said the eagle, "but it's a long way. You must climb the mountain. Keep going uphill. You may see paths that look easier - but they will lead you the wrong way. This way is steep - but it will take you where you want to go."

Dopey sat down and ate his food. He was happy that he was on the right path. He set off again, singing:

Here we come - puff, puff,

On and on - puff, puff,

We won't stop -puff, puff

To the top - puff, puff, puff.

The little dragon pulled himself up the steep slopes. His breathing came in big, deep breaths - in...out, in...out, in...out. The muscles of his legs felt strong and warm. He could feel them tensing up - and relaxing with every step he took. Tense...relax, tense...relax, tense...relax. He was getting higher up the mountain with every step - breath in...out, in...out.

His heart was pumping blood around his body, and as he climbed, his little heart beat faster and faster. He could feel it pounding away in his chest, strong and regular.

Dopey came to a high ledge and stopped to look at the view. He was panting a little by now, but as stopped and rested, his breathing slowed down. He felt his heart slow down too.

He gazed out at the fields below him. The scent of cut grass wafted up to his nose – and he sneezed! The smell reminded him of playing in the garden- it seemed a long time ago. Below him, the eagle circled, his wings almost still as he glided on the warm air currents.

Dopey began to feel sleepy. This was something he was very, very good at! He had come a long way – time for a nap! Dopey lay down and was soon fast asleep.

As Dopey lay dreaming, a little fly came by. It buzzed in Dopey's ear.

"Time to get up," said the fly. "You've a long way to go."

Dopey woke up and stretched. He stretched every muscle in his body; he yawned and got to his feet.

He could see the top of the mountain, but it was still a long way off. He pushed on, up and up. And up. And up.

His legs ached. His breathing came in gasps. His heart beat faster and faster. He felt hotter and hotter.

At last, he reached the top – but it wasn't really the top at all! There was another top further away. Dopey was disappointed – but being a brave little dragon, he stumbled on, further and further.

He was tired and thirsty, and the sun was going down. It was getting darker and darker. He was feeling a little bit afraid.

And then the moon shone out – full of face and smiling down at Dopey. It lit up a magical world. The rocks gleamed in the pale moonlight. A little stream appeared almost under his feet, and Dopey drank the cool water.

The path was still rough and steep, but Dopey felt stronger now. His muscles were moving well, his heart was beating powerfully, and his breathing was in time with his steps. Ahead he saw a little cave, lit up by the pale moon. The entrance looked safe and welcoming.

The little dragon lay down on the sandy floor by the cave entrance. He was too tired to explore further – he had earned a rest.

As he lay there, he looked up at the bright stars in the velvet darkness of the sky. They looked like jewels. Some gleamed red, others a brilliant pale blue, and still others white and bright, and all of them beautiful. He wondered if any dragons lived on the stars?

As he rested, his heart slowed down, he could feel it beating steadily in his chest. If he listened carefully, he could just hear it as it pumped away – boom de boom...boom de boom...boom de boom.

His breathing slowed down, in and out, softly hardly stirring the air. In...out, in...out, in...out...

His muscles relaxed. First, his legs went all soft and heavy. Then his arms went all soft and heavy. The soft feeling spread to his body, his wings drooped, and his neck felt soft and heavy. Finally, his face felt soft, and his mouth relaxed, half-open, and he began to snore, ever so quietly. His eyelids drooped, and soon the little dragon was fast asleep.

The moon passed across the skies. The stars shone as they wheeled across the heavens, and Dopey slept on and on and on.

Dopey the Dreamy Dragon Marches On

Dopey woke from a lovely dream. He was dreaming about a family of dragons –all looking for him. They had a cozy cave, plenty of food, and the sun was shining all the time. Trees and bushes, green, blue, and golden. High cliffs with caves dotted in them. There were streets with dragon shops, a dragon band playing dragon music, and his mommy and daddy and sisters were all with him.

But when Dopey woke up, it was raining – and it was cold – and he was hungry. He had eaten all his sandwiches yesterday. But he knew he had to follow this path to find Dragon Land. So, he set off, a little bit stiff, a little bit wet – and getting wetter – and very hungry.

Soon he came to a rocky place where the path went steeply up, but there was another grassy path leading gently down to the left. On this path, a maiden stood, holding a tray of sausages, beans, and fried potatoes. It looked so good and the little dragon paused to sniff. It smelled so good.

"If you come with me, you can have all you want to eat," said the maiden. "It's not far down this easy path."

Dopey stopped. He smelled the food. He looked at the grassy path. He so much wanted those big fat sausages. But he remembered what the eagle had said. "Keep on the path and don't stray if you want to get to Dragon land."

He carried on up the steep, stony path, and the maiden turned into an ugly witch. She screamed after him. But soon, the little dragon had left her far behind.

After a while, he came to a place where the path was wiggly and twisty. There were sharp corners, and it seemed that he would have to walk a long way to get just a little ways. The ground between corners looked green and easy to walk on, and the path was very clear. He couldn't get lost – could he?

"I'll take a shortcut," thought Dopey. He started to walk across the green grass.

Soon the ground became softer and softer, and he was sinking into the wet ground with every step he took. As he squelched along, he was finding it harder and harder to lift his feet out of the oozy mud – and when he did, the smell was horrible.

The shortcut wasn't working out. He did manage to get back onto the right path, but it had been very tiring, and he was very muddy. He had thought he would never escape. The shortcut had been a disaster!

He continued along the stony path. He felt tired and lonely. He wondered if he would ever get to Dragon Land.

Then he heard music. It was such a happy sound. He heard laughter and singing and wished he could join in. A wide, straight lane opened to his right. Should he go and see where the music was coming from?

Dopey stopped. He thought. Then he remembered his dream, the dream about the dragon family and their cozy cave. He remembered the warm feeling he had in the dream, of being loved and cared for.

He took a big breath, and trying is best not to listen, he hastened on up the stony path.

It wasn't long before the music and laughter faded away. He had his own little song to sing. So, he sang, and that cheered him up.

Here we come - puff, puff,
On and on - puff, puff,
We won't stop -puff, puff,
To the top - puff, puff, puff.

Quite soon, the sun came out; he found some blackberries, and the red juice ran down his face as he ate them. They tasted sweet and tart at the same time.

Then, in the distance, Dopey saw a big, high wall barring his way. On the wall was a door - a very big door. It was closed.

Dopey went closer, and he saw that there was a bell with a rope. He wondered what would happen if he rang the bell. He hoped there wasn't a witch, a goblin, or an ogre. He felt a little bit afraid. His legs felt like jelly, and his mouth felt dry and sandy. He gathered up his courage and took a deep breath. He pulled the rope, and the bell rang out loud and cleared. Dopey wondered who would come?

The door opened, just a crack. Then it opened wide, and the dragon inside said, "Welcome, Dopey. We have been waiting for you."

Dopey went through the door. On the other side was the land he had been dreaming about. Trees and bushes, green, blue, and golden. High cliffs with caves dotted in them. There were streets with dragon shops; a dragon band was playing dragon instruments - the music seemed familiar to Dopey - just like in his dream. He had arrived in Dragon Land.

The dragon who had been guarding the gate led Dopey into the street. And then he heard the most magical sound he had ever heard. "Dopey - my little dragon, we wondered where you were. What have you been doing? Where have you been?" It was the voice of his mommy and daddy.

Dopey told them how he had got lost and couldn't find his way home. He told how he had been looked after by a nice lady and a little girl called Jenny and how he had grown too big for the cat flap.

He told how he had dreamed of Dragon Land. He told them about his long journey – and then he told them he was hungry!

While Dopey had been telling them about his adventures, other dragons were preparing a party to welcome Dopey home. The dragons all brought gifts of food, and a huge table was set up in the street. Bowls and dishes of dragon food were laid out, and glasses of juice to drink. Dopey had never smelled such a wonderful smell as the food at the dragon party. He sat by his mommy and daddy dragon and ate and talked...and ate and talked... and ate and... soon his head was nodding until – plop - it went straight into his dinner plate. He was so tired he had fallen fast asleep at the table.

Now, daddy dragon picked him up, and his mommy dragon cleaned him up. And Dopey dreamed on. They tucked him up in a dragon bed in their cozy cave. Dopey's dream had come true. He was home at last.

The Dreamy Dragon Masters His Nightmare

Dopey, the dreamy dragon, was fast asleep. But his eyes were flickering behind his closed lids. Dopey was dreaming.

But it wasn't a nice dream. Oh, no! Dopey was having a nightmare, and Dopey was very frightened,

He was dreaming that he was lost on a dark pathway through a forest. The trees were thick and leaning over towards Dopey, threatening on either side. The path was faint, and he wasn't sure whether he should keep going or turn back. In fact, Dopey was lost.

All at once, in the distance, he saw two small lights on the path. Dopey hurried towards them.

"They must be people with torches; they could help me," he thought.

But as he got closer, he saw that the lights were the red, glowing eyes of a fearsome beast. The beast saw Dopey and started to lumber towards him. It came slowly at first and then faster and faster. The earth shook as the beast pounded on. Dopey was terrified. The beast was almost upon him. He could feel the hot air of his breath and the smell of his sweat...At that moment, he woke up.

His mommy was right beside him, stroking his face. She leaned over him, and he could smell her delicate scent.

"It's all right, little dragon," she said, "You were just dreaming."

She asked him about his dream, and he told her a fearsome beast was chasing him in a dark forest - and he was lost.

His mommy said, "Tell me - if you could escape - how would you do it?"

Dopey thought about it for a few moments. He realized that there were cables high up overhead. He could fly up onto them and look down on the fearsome beast. He could fly, but the beast could not. Then, he could run along with the cables, out of the forest, and back home.

"That sounds like a good ending," said his mommy. "Now go to sleep, and if the lights appear on the road, and you see the fearsome beast, you will know how to escape."

The little dragon lay back and closed his eyes. His little chest rose and fell, and he started to go back to sleep. He dropped off- straight into the dark forest. The forest was as scary as before, and in the distance, he saw the lights. But this time, he knew he could fly up onto the cables and escape - but the beast was coming closer and closer and - Dopey woke up again.

This time, he wasn't quite so frightened. In fact, he almost wanted to go back into the dream. This time he would sit on the cables and laugh at the fearsome beast.

But it was time to get up. A new day was breaking. The fearsome beast would have to wait.

That day, the lessons at school were all about how to fly and use their wings to power through the air. Dopey listened with great care. His wings were growing nicely. He felt he could flap them. He felt a rush of air above and under them as he beat his wings. Soon he as flying up with all his little friends. Up above the schoolyard, up into the air. It was the best lesson ever!

That playtime, all the dragons were practicing flying. Some of them were still fluttering just about the yard. Some were going quite high in the sky, and the teacher had to call them back. Dopey was dreaming, as usual. He flew out over the sea and far away. He flew among the clouds and looked down on their sunlit cotton wool tops.

He loved the feel of flying. The cool air, the way he could see so far. He loved the strong pull of his muscles as he beat his wings. He tasted the salty tang of the sea air and licked his lips.

That woke him up, and he realized he was far out to sea. It was time to turn around and find his schoolyard again. He turned around and flew back. But where was the schoolyard?

Dopey was getting worried - he shouldn't have flown so far away. But then he thought - *well, I can fly. I can fly a long way, but I must learn to remember the way!*

At that moment, he saw far below him the street where he lived - and his mommy was just hanging the wash on the line. Then, it was easy to follow the street back to school. He landed with a bit of a bump.

"Landings still needed practice," he thought.

Soon Dopey was back in class. He felt very confident that he could fly - fly as far as he wanted to - and even learn to find his way home again.

That night, Dopey fell asleep as soon as his head touched the pillow. It had been a tiring day - all that flying. As he drifted off to sleep, he thought about how well he could fly, how lovely the feeling was up in the sky, cool air, fresh scents, little clouds to play among...

And then he found himself back in the dark forest. But this time, he was happy to fly up above the trees. He hovered in the sky, waiting to see the fearsome beast. As expected, it came, thundering along the pathway.

"What are you doing up there, little dragon?" it growled.

"I'm flying - you can never catch me now."

The fearsome beast looked up at him. "But I only wanted to play," it said.

The dragon thought that was odd; he had seemed so fierce – but now he seemed as if he might be fun.

"Tomorrow night," said Dopey, and promptly fell into a deep, dreamless sleep.

The next night, after he had been practicing his flying, Dopey wanted to dream about the beast. He wasn't so fearsome after all. His last thought before he entered the land of dreams was – "Come and play, funny beasty, come out and play with me tonight."

Very soon, Dopey was back in the forest. The sun seemed to be shining in his sleep. The trees were lit up with golden light. The beast appeared – and pretended to be fierce, but it wanted to play, just like Dopey.

The two played among the trees. Every now and then, Dopey flew up above the beast. Every now and then, the beast nearly caught the little dragon – but he never did. Dopey wasn't frightened at all. He was having fun.

The two played most of the night in Dopey's dreams. He had found that a fearsome beast wasn't always as fierce as he thought – and he had found he could control his dream. He could even look forward to having his nightmare since he had the power to change it – all by himself.

Dopey the Dreamy Dragon Learns to Control His Fire

Dopey was growing into a fine young dragon. He had learned to fly, and he loved flying high among the clouds. He darted between them and chased around them. He dreamed of being a knight in armor. He dreamed of being the biggest cloud in the sky. He swooped and glided his big wings outstretched, feeling the cool air passing over him. He smelled the rain as it gently washed over him. He was really good at flying.

But he was having trouble with breathing fire.

As you know, all dragons can breathe out fire. They do it when they are angry. They do it when they want to dry out the caves where they live. They breathe out fire to cook and to make patterns on the sky as they dance. There are lots of useful things they can do when they breathe out fire. But they must breathe it out in the right way.

And Dopey just wasn't getting it.

Every morning he wanted toast for breakfast - and every morning, without fail - he burnt it. The first sound his friends would hear every morning was the sound of Dopey scraping the burnt bits off his toast.

When Dopey wanted to dry his cave, all the other dragons rushed to get out of the way. They thought this was rather a nuisance and grumbled. But Dopey just couldn't get it right.

And although Dopey was one of the very best dancers in the sky, his fire patterns were either too bright or almost invisible.

What could Dopey do?

He practiced - and all the other dragons kept far away. But one of the older dragons had been watching him. He knew that Dopey might be dreamy, but he was also a determined little dragon. The old dragon decided to help him.

"Dopey," he said. "You need to relax. "Breathing isn't difficult, and breathing fire is just a special kind of breathing."

"I have another special kind of breathing, just to help you relax." Said the old dragon. "I call it 'square breathing.'"

Dopey thought that was a silly name - *who ever heard of square breathing*? But he was a polite little dragon, and he knew that sometimes - not always - older dragons were wiser than he was. So, he listened carefully and did exactly what the old dragon said.

"This is how you do it:
Breathe in and count to four - one, two, three, four.
Hold it for four counts - one, two, three, four.
Breathe out for four counts - one, two, three, four.
And hold it for four counts - one, two, three, four.
Repeat this four times, and you will feel relaxed and ready to start doing something you might have found to be difficult before."

Dopey tried it. He did feel a little less tense. He wanted to try it again, but the old dragon said, "Four times are enough. Like most good things, you can do too much."

Now it was time to try it out. He took a piece of bread, and, very carefully, he blew on it. Nothing happened. He thought about flames and... very gently... he blew again. This time a small flame came out with his breath - and the bread was toasted to perfection. Dopey was very pleased.

The next day Dopey did his square breathing just once - he felt relaxed and blew on the bread for breakfast - and he ended up with a nice brown piece of toast. The other dragons were waiting to hear the sound of Dopey scraping his burnt toast; they waited in vain.

Now it was time for a bigger flame. Dopey wanted to dry out the cave where he was sleeping.

The old dragon smiled to himself. Dopey was dreamy - but he was determined and used his mind to control the way he made fire. He needed to concentrate. He needed to think. He needed to clear his mind.

Dopey took two square breathes. He felt relaxed. Tasking another big breath, he breathed into the cave. It wasn't a perfect breathe, but it did dry out the cave without setting anything on fire. Dopey was pleased. The other dragons were amazed!

Dopey felt happy - it was time to dance in the skies. Just before he set off, he took a big relaxing breath, and as he did, he felt himself breathing in the sense of control. He was confident he could make fire as he danced among the clouds. He just needed to relax and think about it. This wasn't a time to go off dreaming and forgetting everything.

Dopey took off into the skies. He breathed in deeply and then blew out slowly, and as he did, the fire came out of his mouth - just as it should with a dragon. He blew patterns in the sky as he weaved his way among the clouds. He still had to concentrate. He had to breathe with deep, slow breaths.

The other dragons joined him. And they all flew about the skies, making fiery patterns as they danced.

Dopey loved being a dragon. He loved the feel of his powerful wings beating the air and the coolness as the air passed over his body. He loved the clean smell of the clouds and the misty damp on his skin as he played among them.

Dopey loved the breathing trick, which helped him relax and then made it easier for him to do anything he wanted. He could make toast, he could dry the cave - and he could make fiery patterns in the sky.

The old dragon watched Dopey and smiled to himself. "Control your breathing," he thought. "And you can relax enough to tackle anything."

Chapter 2: Una the Ultra-Sonic Unicorn Yarns

How Una the Unicorn Found Friends

Once upon a time, in a far-off place, there was an enchanted forest.

Amongst the trees lived the fairies, the pixies, the dwarves, and the elves. Dancing between the trees was a herd of horses. There also lived a unicorn, who was very lonely.

The horses wouldn't play with her – because she was different. She had a horn.

The fairies wouldn't play with her because they said she was ugly, the pixies teased her, the dwarves wanted nothing to do with her. The elves, who were neither here nor there, simply ignored her.

She would go out each day hoping someone would play with her, but no one ever did. She would watch the other horses, and the tears poured down her cheeks. She was a very sad little unicorn.

But she was kind and generous. She would have been the best of friends, if only the fairies, or the pixies, or the dwarves or the elves, who were neither here nor there, would let her. And especially if the other horses would let her join in their games and be part of their herd.

Near to the enchanted forest lived a little girl whose name was Lily. Her mother had told her never to go into the enchanted forest - who knows what might be there? But Lily, although she was usually a very good little girl, was curious about the forest and she could be naughty sometimes.

The more she was told never to enter the woods, the more curious she became. One day, when the sun was hot - and she was tired of playing in her garden, she decided to explore the woods. She wanted to shelter from the sun under the trees.

She crossed the field to the forest and ran in under the trees. After a little while, she felt cool and a little bit nervous. She wasn't quite sure of the way out - everywhere she looked, there were trees. She stopped, and it all seemed very quiet...

The fairies had fled when the little girl came walking into their forest. The dwarves had hidden underground, even the gay pixies had run laughing quietly to the very tops of the trees. The elves were both here and there, as usual. The little unicorn peered round the biggest tree she could find, the tears streaming down over his nose.

As Lily walked on, all by herself, she heard a muffled sobbing sound. She gazed around but saw nothing except trees - and more trees. Yet the sobbing sound continued and seemed to come from behind a huge old oak tree. She looked around it - and saw the little unicorn's horn sticking out from behind the tree. She was crying so much and looked so sad.

Lily stopped and reached out a gentle hand. "Why are you crying?" she asked.

"No one wants to play with me. Every day I am all alone," replied the unicorn, sniffing.

Lily found a tissue and gave it to her. "I'll play with you," she said.

The two played all afternoon. They played *tiggy* and *chasey*, and *guess what I am*. They played hiding behind the trees and catching the leaves and seeking for treasure. They played so much and laughed so much that their sides were aching as the evening drew near.

All this time, the fairies were watching, the pixies looking down, the dwarves peeking from behind stones, and the elves taking notice wherever they were. And the horses peeped round the trees, amazed. They all wanted to join in the games, but they were a little afraid of the girl. They thought the unicorn was very brave - and she seemed to be having such fun.

As the sun began to go down, the woods started to get darker. Lily suddenly remembered that she had a home to go to - and she had no idea where she was. "Don't worry," said the unicorn, "I'll take you right to the edge to the wood."

With her hand tucked into her mane, the little girl and the unicorn ran through the trees till they came to the edge of the forest.

Lily could see her house across the field, the lights shone from the windows, and she heard her mother calling. Lightly she ran across the field, and the unicorn watched her go. She felt a little sad that she was by himself again but very happy to have had such a wonderful afternoon.

As she started on her way home, a little fairy came out from behind a tree and shyly asked her if he would play with her tomorrow. Then the other fairies came out of hiding, begging her to play with them, too. The pixies flew down for the tree-tops and joined in. The dwarves came up from the ground, and even the elves, who were neither here nor there, were dancing around and asking the little unicorn to play with them.

And the horses wanted her to join their herd. They gathered around the little unicorn and gently nudged her and blew kisses at her the way horses do. They all wanted to be close to the little unicorn. She was so brave - and such fun.

From that day to this, the little unicorn was never lonely anymore - there were always fairies, pixies, or dwarves or even the elves wanting to play with her - and sometimes, all of them at once. And the horses welcomed her into their herd, to be like one of them. She became a very happy little unicorn. But most of all, she knew she belonged to the herd of horses.

She might be different- but that made her special. And the horses realized that although she did look unique, inside, she was just like themselves. She could laugh, play, and tell terrible jokes – just like they could.

And as for Lily? She thought she had been sleeping and had had the most wonderful dream.

Her friends returned from their holidays, and Lily had plenty of children to play with. She was a happy little girl, no longer curious about the enchanted forest. Sometimes, when she was by herself, she would think of her special dream place and the friendly unicorn and feel happy.

Una and Jeremy Save the Little Unicorn

It was nighttime in the forest. The sun had sunk behind the trees, and shadows were stealing through the leaves. The wood took on a secret, dark look. There were deep hollows and peaceful quiet. Everyone was asleep.

Una, the Ultra-Sonic Unicorn, was resting after playing all day with the horses. She heard a soft "whoo, whoo," from the owl; she heard the soft pattering beneath the trees as the tiny mice went about their business.

Gradually, she realized that she heard another sound - a sound she had never heard before. It was a bit like the rush of water falling in a waterfall. But not quite. It was like the urgent whispering of the leaves before a storm. But not quite.

What was it? Una decided to find out.

She trotted off toward the noise. It seemed a long way off. As she got closer, she could hear that it was an animal in distress, and she galloped towards the sound. Then she saw the back end of a pony, struggling and pulling in the bushes. She heard the pony crying and panting. He was very, very stuck.

Una knew that she couldn't free him herself – she needed help. And she knew where to get it!

She had a friend, a little boy called Jeremy. He could free the poor little pony.

Jeremy lived in a little house in the country. They had a garden, and in the garden was an old apple tree. The tree was a favorite place for Jeremy; in the winter, he could see the branches black against the grey sky. When Spring came, he would watch the tiny green buds gradually grow and magically burst open.

In summer, he could lie in the shade and gaze up at the pattern the leaves made against the blue sky, and, of course, his favorite time was autumn, when the apples would drop off onto the lawn – and Jeremy would eat them!

One autumn, after all the apples had been picked from the tree, Jeremy's daddy set up a swing. He took a piece of strong wood and fixed it to stout ropes, which he hung from a high branch in the apple tree. Jeremy loved his swing, sometimes he would swing as high as he could, and other days he just sat there and dreamed, gently rocking to and fro.

That autumn, the skies were clear, and the air was cold. At nighttime, the world seemed to turn into a white wonderland, the trees rimed with frost, and even in Jeremy's warm bedroom, the windows had leafy patterns.

One night, Jeremy just couldn't sleep. He gazed out of his window as the full moon shone brightly, the very air seemed as if magic was around.

Jeremy put on his warm dressing gown and his slippers. He felt excited and not at all cold as he crept downstairs and quietly opened the back door and walked across the lawn to the apple tree, his feet crunching the white frost and leaving dark footprints across the grass.

The swing hung, seeming to be waiting for Jeremy. He sat down, and the swing began to sway, and rock, and swing higher and higher all by itself. Suddenly Jeremy found himself swinging high into the air and away from the apple tree into the clear dark skies.

The swing seemed to know where it was going, so fast, and so high. Jeremy looked down at the village street and gardens, all lit by the bright, full moon. And the stars sparkled as he passed them by.

After a while, they started to descend as they came to a forest of silver trees. And this is where he had met Una. They became friends, and very occasionally, he would visit her.

Una knew she had to fetch Jeremy. She knew where he lived, and she set off at a gallop. She ran fast; her hooves barely grazed the ground. Soon she reached Jeremy's house. It was in darkness; all the lights were off.

Standing up on her hind legs, Una tapped on his bedroom window. Jeremy just turned over and muttered in his sleep. She tapped again, harder. Jeremy woke up. He realized someone was tapping at his window- and they would break it, they were not careful. He slipped out of his warm bed and went to the window.

He was surprised to see Una there. She begged him to hurry. He put on his dressing-gown and tiptoed downstairs carrying his shoes. Then he ran to the apple tree and started to swing - up and down, up and down, up and away.

The swing, with Jeremy holding on tight, followed Una. Soon they came to the forest. The swing dropped down into a clearing, and Jeremy stood up, looking around him at the trees and the tall, thick thorny undergrowth around him.

He heard a scrabbling sound and heavy breathing nearby, and the bushes seemed to be moving and thrashing around in one place. He moved closer and realized that a large animal was trapped and was trying desperately to free himself.

Jeremy went nearer and saw it was a little white horse, and his head was fixed in the bushes - going even nearer, he spoke gently to the horse. To his amazement, the horse spoke back, saying, " My horn is stuck, and I cannot free it, please help me."

So, Jeremy took some big steps toward the horse's head - and sure enough, there was a long straight horn tangled up in the bushes. The unicorn stood still, panting, as Jeremy unwound the wicked thorns and, after a struggle, managed to free the little unicorn.

They stood and looked at each other in the forest glade, the unicorn calmer now. Jeremy, with scratches in his hands which he never noticed, was so intent was he gazed at the unicorn - there really was a horn!

The moon looked down from the sky. The shadows were getting longer as the moon slowly got lower until it was just peeping over the trees.

The swing rested quietly, but the little unicorn said, "Thank you so much, thank you. Now I must get you safely home. Jump on my back and bring the swing with you. But we must be quick because when the full moon goes down, I will lose my horn and turn back into an ordinary horse."

Una watched them go. She was so happy that the little unicorn was saved. All that galloping had been hard work, but well worthwhile.

The unicorn sped through the trees and across the fields, its feet hardly touching the ground. Jeremy hung onto its thick mane and laughed for joy. It felt so exciting; he felt so happy. All too soon, they arrived back in the garden, and the swing left Jeremy's arms and replaced itself in the apple tree.

Jeremy climbed off the back of the unicorn. He thanked him again for saving him and told him that when the moon was full, some – but not all – horses could become unicorns. They were only unicorns while the moon was in the sky. But in the daytime, they were just ordinary horses. You really couldn't tell which horses would be unicorns when the moon came up.

Swiftly, the little unicorn flew away with a happy neigh. Jeremy crept upstairs to his nice warm bed. But ever after, when he saw horses anywhere, he would wonder whether they became unicorns when the moon was full.

Una the Unicorn Stops Showing Off

In the enchanted forest, all the creatures were looking forward to the midnight party. It didn't happen very often – only when the moon turned blue. They knew that the next night there would be a blue moon.

Everyone was preparing – food, drink, and what to wear.

The horses were bringing great heaps of clean hay and fresh-cut grass.

The fairies were making tiny fairy cakes with every color you can think of. They added sparkly dots to the tops; they did look pretty.

The pixies oversaw the drinks – orange, pineapple, blueberry, and, of course, fresh water.

The dwarves provided plates of gold and silver drinking vessels.

No one knew what the elves would bring – they were never about when you wanted to ask them.

But what was Una the Ultra-Sonic Unicorn to bring? She wanted something special, something unique.

She borrowed a basket from a kind fairy and hung it on her horn. And then she went looking for something good to eat.

First, she found some wild strawberries. There were not many, but she put what she found into her basket - they were sweet and tangy. Going on a little further, she found the blackberry bushes - she almost filled her basket with big, juicy, sweet berries.

But she wanted something extra special. She went deeper into the forest; it was getting darker and darker the further she went. The trees were crowding together, and the leaves overhead were whispering to each other. Little patches of the forest floor were lit up by the sun - but not very many. Una thought she had better go back and rejoin the herd.

Just as she was about to leave the deep dark forest, she heard a tiny voice, somewhere down by her hooves.

"What are you looking for?" the little voice said.

Una looked down. "I want something special for the party." She said.

"I know a bank where the wild carrots grow," said the tiny voice. "But I can't reach them. If you pick one for me, you can pick a few more."

Una looked down. There, half-hidden by the fallen leaves, she saw a small, tiny mouse. The mouse twitched her tiny whiskers and, followed by her tiny tail, ran lightly through the crackling leaves.

Una followed her.

They came to a forest glade that Una had never visited before. The sun shone through, making dappled patterns on the ground beneath. Through the middle, there flowed a sparkling stream.

And there on a bank, the wild carrots grew.

Una was delighted - all horses loved carrots, and these were big and juicy - and amazing colors. She crunched one up. It felt firm as she bit down...

She knew she would have to run back to be in time for the party.

"Please," said the tiny mouse, "May I come too?"

"Jump on my back," said Una.

But the mouse was too small. She couldn't jump so high.

Una knelt and lowered her head. The little mouse was able to clamber up Una's horn and nestled in her mane. Una set off at a gallop. The tiny mouse gripped hard and held on tightly. The wind rushed past her tiny face and ruffled her whiskers. She had never gone fast.

Soon they were back at the party. Una proudly put her basket with the few sweet strawberries, the blackberries, and the big juicy carrots on the table. She felt so proud. The tiny mouse climbed down and looked about her.

She saw the pretty fairy cakes - and had a little nibble they tasted light and fluffy. She admired the little golden plate the dwarf gave her and drank a little pineapple juice from a tiny silver cup.

The elves appeared, carrying bags of nuts and spicy sorrel leaves. Everyone was enjoying the party.

Una thought that her offering was the best; she had brought the best berries and the biggest carrots.

"See the berries - lots and lots of them," she said

And they all looked

"Look at my juicy carrots," she said.

And they all looked.

Then they turned away and started to chatter among themselves. They didn't like Una boasting. They had all brought their best offers - why did she have to think she was the best?

After a while, Una felt a little sad. The light seemed dimmer, the party noisy, and the air chillier. No one was speaking to her, and she felt very left out.

Then the tiny mouse squeaked at her for the tabletop. "I helped you - tell them about me," she said.

Una looked at her. She was right. She had told her about the wild bank where the carrots grew. Maybe she should listen to the fairies and tell them how good their cakes tasted?

So, she did.

And the fairies listened and were pleased.

"Perhaps now I should congratulate the dwarves on their beautiful plates and cups?" she thought.

So, she did.

And the dwarves were pleased to be praised. It didn't happen very often, and they had spent a long time polishing them until they gleamed.

"Maybe I should tell the pixie how much I enjoyed their juice when I was so thirsty?"

So, she did.

And the pixies were pleased; it had been heavy to carry all that juice.

She told the horses how much she had enjoyed tucking into the fresh-cut grass. And they were happy.

And then she thought, "I'll tell everyone about the tiny mouse," so she did.

The tiny mouse was shy and hid her tiny face – but the elves stroked her, and the pixies comforted her, and all the creatures gave her much attention. The tiny mouse was the star of the party. And Una felt warm inside. It was so much better to listen and praise than to boast about herself.

Una realized that she was liked when she listened to others rather than talk about herself all the time. She would make friends more easily; she didn't need to boast.

The party went on most of the night. The blue moon faded and began to leave the sky. The stars went out. The whole sky began to get a little lighter. Dawn was coming,

Una knew she had to take the tiny mouse back to her home in the dark part of the forest. The tiny mouse climbed up Una's horn and nestled amongst her mane. Una set off, trotting through the early morning forest. The birds woke up and started to sing. The night owl went to sleep in his high treetop hole, and the creatures of the forest prepared for another day.

Una took the tiny mouse all the way back to the deep, dark place where she had her home. The tiny mouse would sleep all day and dream of the wonderful party,

Una made her way safely back to her home with the herd of horsed she lived with, and the fairies, the pixies, the dwarves, and the elves.

She was content. She had learned that listening is sometimes better than talking, that praising others was better than boasting about yourself.

She had found her friends were more interesting than she had realized. She quietly she made her way back along the forest track. Soon she was home; soon, it was time to rest.

She lay down and stretched out. She closed her eyes. She breathed slowly and quietly, every breath going deeper and deeper. Her heart slowed down as she rested going be-boom, be-boom, be-boom softly in her chest. What a busy night!

As she lay there, she remembered all the things she had seen. She thought of all the things she had heard. She smelled the fresh-cut grass; she imagined tasting the fairy cakes again. She thought of the tiny mouse snug in its home, and very soon she was fast asleep – smiling, as unicorns who are happy do smile in their sleep.

Una and the Patchwork Quilt

Una and the herd of wild horses were drifting thought the forest, wondering what to do. They had plenty of food, but the weather was getting colder as Autumn was creeping into Winter. The leaves were many colors – green still, but also brown and golden and a deep rich red. They rustled under hoof, and the horses were kicking them up and watching them swirl away in the light breeze.

Then Una, with her ultra-sonic hearing, heard something else. Something that made her pause...

It sounded a little like a sighing – was it just the wind? She played on, but the sound came again. What was it? She needed to find out.

So, she left the playing horses and trotted towards the edge of the enchanted forest. She didn't come this way very often.

As she neared the open fields, she saw a little donkey. I looked exhausted and sad. Its head was drooping, and it was shivering. Sometimes it let out a soft, sad sigh... as if it was too tired to make much noise.

Una went up to the little donkey. "What's the matter?" she asked.

"My master said I was too old to work anymore, so he sent me off to find my own way. And I am lost, and hungry and so, so tired," said the little donkey.

Una felt very sorry for the poor little donkey.

"Don't worry," she said. "You can come with me to the enchanted forest, and we'll look after you."

So, the little donkey followed Una back into the forest under the Autumn leaves. As they walked along, the fairies peeked out, and seeing the tired little donkey, they fluttered around her and looked so pretty that the tired little donkey felt a little less tired.

Then the pixies had to come and see. They told the little donkey terrible jokes, which made her laugh – the first laugh she had had for a very long time. Soon the dwarves came, and even the elves – who were neither here nor there – came and went and helped the little donkey on her way.

All the creatures made the little donkey feel welcome. They found water for her and the best fresh hay. They cheered her up with terrible jokes and funny stories. But still, she was shivering. "I'm cold," she said. "Winter is on its way, and I have no rug to cover me as once I did."

One of the fairies said – "I'll knit you a blanket of gossamer," and she set to work. Soon she had knitted a beautiful blanket of gossamer. But the fairy was small, and the blanket was tiny. It wouldn't even cover the donkey's ear.

The other fairies saw what was happening, and they all said they would each knit a square to cover more of the donkey. And they did. Soon there a hundred beautiful gossamer squares. The only trouble was – they were all separate. They would all blow away and wouldn't stay on the donkey.

Una had an idea. "Why not sew the squares together?" she suggested.

The pixies offered to do this. They asked the spiders if they could use some silk from their webs. The spiders were pleased to be asked to help. Soon all the squares were joined, making a lovely patchwork of colored squares, each one a different color. But it was very fragile.

"It needs a strong border," said Una.

"We can make a strong border," said the dwarves. We'll weave it out of grass and hay. So, they wove a strong border. It looked beautiful.

Just one thing to make it perfect," said Una. "It needs a soft lining so that it feels as good as it looks."

Now the elves had been watching all this, sometimes here, sometimes there. "We'll make the lining," they cried.

They darted up into the sky and gathered the fluffy white clouds to make the fluffiest, softest lining you can imagine. The sun smiled down as they gathered up the fluffy white clouds.

The patchwork quilt was ready. Everyone had helped to make it; the fairies had knitted the squares of gossamer. The pixies had joined them together with the silk from the webs of spiders. The dwarves had made the edges strong with grass and hay, and the elves had lined it with soft white clouds.

That night the little donkey settled down in her new patchwork coat of many colors. It felt so soft and warm. She wasn't shivering anymore. She gave a big sigh of contentment. She had a new home. She had new friends. She had a place she could call home. She was a very happy, very sleepy little donkey.

The elves were happy, too. They had helped all the creatures of the forest make something very special. The lining was perfect. Together something fine had been created. They couldn't have done it all by themselves. The disappeared and - if elves rest, then that is what they did.

The dwarves were happy, too. They knew that if they hadn't made a strong edging, the beautiful quilt would not have lasted. They had had an important part to play. The soon snuggled down and went snoring off the land of dreams.

The pixies were happy, too. They had asked the spiders help – and the spiders were pleased to think of their fine silken thread was holding the patchwork squares together. It can be good to ask for help. Soon the pixies were asleep.

The fairies were happy, too. They had had the idea of knitting the squares, and each of them had made something beautiful. It was so good to work together. Soon the fairies were fast asleep.

Una lay awake for a long time. The little donkey was fast asleep beside her. She felt very peaceful. She had heard the sounds of the little donkey in distress. She had listened carefully to what she heard. And she had gone to make sure that what she heard didn't need help. And she had done what needed to be done.

Everyone had wanted to help. She could not have made a beautiful patchwork quilt herself. Everyone had a part to play. Together they could make wonderful things happen.

She felt at ease with herself. Tired after a busy day, content, and drowsy. She heard the steady sound of the little donkey breathing and matched her own breathing in time, steady and slow...steady...and slow...she stretched out her legs and relaxed them... limp and floppy. She wriggled her neck and relaxed...limp and floppy...she breathed in slowly and out...slowly...slowly...slowly, her eyes closed. Soon Una was in the land of dreams, fast asleep.

Una the Unicorn Finds Peace

Una the unicorn woke up one misty morning with a slight headache. The sounds of the other horses in her herd seemed loud and noisy. When they laughed with a ringing neigh, she felt her head would burst. Even the sound of them chomping the grass for breakfast made her feel a little bit irritated.

She decided to go for a calming, gentle walk all by herself; Una liked being with her friends - but just occasionally, she wanted to be alone. She knew she could come back whenever she wanted to.

She slowly walked to the edge of the clearing and drifted among the trees. She wasn't rushing. She wasn't looking for anything particular. She wasn't in a hurry; she had all the time in the world.

Slowly, she paced on her little hooves stepping daintily along the path. She felt the ground underneath, firm yet soft, but strong to support her.

She felt her slow breathing and breathed in the smells of the forest. The leaves were just beginning to fall, the grassy path she was treading on had a light, grassy scent. She caught the occasional scent of wildflowers - honeysuckle's sweet smell carried for a short time on the still air. The air felt damp, and as she peered through the mist, the trees seemed to have become less dense, less sturdy.

Una walked on into an older part of the forest. Few creatures came this far into the old forest. It had secret ways and hidden paths, weeds tangled in the undergrowth. The air itself seemed faintly green, in part of the forest with aged, bent trees with lichen hanging from the branches. The mist grew thicker. The air felt heavier. Soon she came to the banks of a river, slow-flowing, sluggishly twisting and turning its way through the trees.

The waters looked black. She gazed down and saw a reflection of herself in the calm river flowing gently past. Looking deeper, she saw the shadows of fish, and deeper down the rounded stones and pebbles lying there.

Una felt a sense of mystery - and a sense that all was well.

After a while, she came to a stone wall - now in ruins. The remains of a person are long gone. The stones were piled around in rough heaps, mossy and soft to look at. She noticed that many of the cracks in the walls had tiny insects making their homes there. It was a good feeling to know that nature was taking back the forest for her own.

She saw that the mist was slowly lifting. Only the tops of the trees were now shrouded in the soft white clouds of mist. Una stopped by a gnarled old oak tree. She rubbed her head against the bark and felt the hard strength of the tree. The power seemed to come from deep within the ground- a sense of power and control. The earth itself was talking to her through the ancient tree. She listened to its wisdom. She felt strong; the tree was giving her power and strength – power from deep within the earth beneath.

She looked up. The branches were reaching up into the mists. As the white mists hung around and then slowly vanished, the twigs and leaves came into view. They looked serene and calm. The branches swayed a little – supple and flexible – just as she was.

She stepped around the ancient oak tree. She found herself in a small glade. There was grass underfoot, and the sun was making patterns on the ground beneath. It seemed to be a very special place. Very peaceful, very calm. The trees and grass were many shades of green, deep and dark in the shadows, light and sunny in the tree-tops, and every shade between.

She listened to the soft sounds of the leaves whispering in the tree-tops. It was almost as if the trees were talking to themselves. She heard her own breathing. Slow and steady... slow and steady. This special place was calming. She rested for a while. She knew that she could return to this magical place at any time, in her thoughts, in her dreams.

She thought about the oak tree – so massive and strong. She closed her eyes. She made an image in her mind: a picture of the tree, and of the glade in the ancient wood – a picture she could take back with her as she returned to the herd in the enchanted forest.

Una retraced her steps. Following the path back to her friends, back to the herd, back to horses, and the noise, and the laughter. She felt strong and calm. Her head was clear and alert. It felt good to be a unicorn and to live in the enchanted forest with her friends.

That night when it was time to sleep, she thought about the ancient oak tree and the sunny glade in the old forest. She created a picture in her mind, and as she did so, a feeling of calm came over her.

She could almost smell the sweet honeysuckle. She breathed in deeply. She legs and body relaxed and went all floppy and loose... floppy and loose... as Una settled into sleeping. Her breaths came deep and slow... deep and slow... deep and slow...her eyelids felt heavy and heavier... heavy and heavier...with a sigh, she closed her eyes. Soon, Una was sleeping... dreaming of the magic glade in the ancient forest.

Chapter 3: The Watery World of the Mystical Mermaids

How Merci Conquered Her Fear

Far, far away, under the deep blue sea, there is a castle in the deepest depths of the Ocean. In the castle live five mermaids, and their names are Merci, Mischief, and Merry, Michelle, and Me.

Of coral is the castle made; the windows are of pearly oyster shells. The roof is of the golden treasure sank beneath the waves. Round the castle is a garden, with fronds of seaweed waving gently in the current. Bright fish of many colors dart amongst the seaweed, like birds amongst our trees. The sandy bottom blooms with sea urchins, starfish, and many other beautiful sea creatures and flowers. The garden is bright with color, reds, and yellows, deep greens and rusty browns all set off against the blue of the moving water.

All the little mermaids had long, flowing hair and jeweled combs. All the little mermaids had twisty, twitchy tails. And all the little mermaids could sing.

But none had so sweet a voice as Merci. When Merci sang, the fishes stopped darting in and out and paused to listen. The droopy octopus came out from his rocky shelter to hear her better. The starfish reached out their many legs to gather the sound, even the ocean's currents stilled, and the sea stood still.

But Merci was shy, and rarely did she sing.

Once every thirteen moon months in the ocean depths, a great festival of singing was held. All the best singers competed for the honor of winning. The winner also won a silver chalice encrusted with red rubies and blue sapphires to keep. But every year, Merci was too shy to enter the competition. And every year, her sisters urged her to try.

"You could win," said Mischief.

"It would make us so happy to hear you sing," cried Merry, looking sad.

"The silver chalice would look splendid in our hallway," said Michelle.

Little Me said nothing; she just looked at Merci with sad, hopeful eyes.

At last, Merci agreed to sing in the next festival – it was still five moon months away – a long time.

In the fifth month, she didn't think about the festival at all.

In the fourth month, she started to sing a little in private.

In the third month, she began to feel jittery. Her tummy felt as if a hundred tiny fish were thrashing about in it.

Only two months to go – and she was worried. Her tail sagged, her hair dragged.

One month – and Merci was a mess. Her breathing was fast and shallow. Her singing died away. Her voice no longer sounded pure and mellow but weak and scratchy. What could she do?

The wise old jellyfish swam slowly by. He saw that Merci needed help. He went up to her and gave her a huge, squishy hug. "I can help you breathe," he said. "And then you will be able to sing once more, as beautiful as ever."

He showed her how to breathe in time with the way he moved; slow, steady pulses. "Just imagine I am breathing for you right inside your chest," he said.

At first, Merci found it strange to think of the wise old jellyfish in her chest, breathing for her. But she was a sensible little mermaid, and she wanted to do well. She took a deep breath and let it out through her mouth. Soon it began to feel natural, and her breathing slowed down. The strong, rhythmic pulses made her breathing strong and deep. She had plenty of air to sing – and the songs began to come again.

Soon the month became weeks, and then days before the festival. Merci found it easier and easier to imagine the wise old jellyfish breathing with her. Whenever she felt nervous, she just imagined him, slowly pulsing his way through the sea, and her breathing calmed down, and she felt stronger and more relaxed.

The day of the festival arrived.

Her sisters helped her dress for the show. Mischief combed her hair till it shone. Merry made her laugh. Michelle gave her lovely, soft pink shell for her hair, and I gave her courage – "You can do it, you can do it," she said.

The stage was set. Shells decorated the edges of the stage. Graceful fronds of seaweed acted as curtains. The orchestra took their places. The deep sound of the conch shells sounded out, the sea cucumbers trumpeted, and the whispery sound of the sea urchins *whissed* as they opened and closed, adding to the music. Everything was ready.

One after another, the mermaids sang. One after another, their voices thrilled the audience. One after another until it was the turn of Merci – the very last mermaid to sing. The judges thought she was too young to sing well. The audience wanted to get to the buffet and eat their fill. Everyone thought she would be nervous, frightened, and that her voice would be weak and wobbly.

Then Merci took a big breath. She started to sing. Her voice rang out, deep, strong, and beautiful.

The judges were amazed. The audience stopped fidgeting. Merci sang on, and the ocean world was still.

When she finished, there was a moment of complete silence – and then the place erupted in cheers and applause.

Merci won the silver chalice, and it did look well in her hallway, and that pleased her.

But what pleased her far more was the way she had dealt with her fear. She knew how to control it. She knew that there would be time ahead when she might feel nervous- but when she imagined the wise old jellyfish breathing with him in her chest, she knew that she could cope with anything.

And the wise old jellyfish? He moved slowly away, pulsing rhythmically as he went, far out into the ocean's distant reaches. He was pleased that he had helped the mermaid with the lovely voice. He had others to help, more to do beneath the waves in the far-off sea.

Maybe one day he will help you. If you ever get a little bit nervous, think of that kind old jellyfish pulsing his way through the seas, strong and rhythmic. And match your breathing to him. You will feel strong, ready for any challenge.

The Mischievous Mermaid Learns to be Kind

Far, far away, under the deep blue sea, there is a castle in the deepest depths of the ocean. In the castle live five mermaids, and their names are Merci, Mischief, and Merry, Michelle, and Me.

Of coral is the castle made; the windows are of pearly oyster shells. The roof is of the golden treasure sank beneath the waves. Round the castle is a garden, with fronds of seaweed waving gently in the current. Bright fish of many colors dart amongst the seaweed, like birds amongst our trees. The sandy bottom blooms with sea urchins, starfish, and many other beautiful sea creatures and flowers. The garden is bright with color, reds, and yellows, deep greens and rusty browns all set off against the blue of the moving water.

All the little mermaids had long, flowing hair and jeweled combs. All the little mermaids had twisty, twitchy tails. And all the little mermaids could tease. But Mischief was the biggest tease - she loved to make mischief.

She used to play jokes on every living thing she could find, and she told the most terrible jokes! Sometimes she went too far. Sometimes her jokes were not very funny.

She especially liked to tease old Grouper of the yellow mouth. He had been around long before Mischief was born, even before her mother was a baby mermaid. He was wise, and he was gentle - but he was old. He couldn't see as well as he used to. He couldn't swim as fast as he used to. He wasn't as strong as he used to be.

He got tired easily, and that made him a little bit grumpy, though he was really a very kind old fish. He just wanted to be left alone, although he needed someone to care for him in his old age.

Mischief would show him a small dull pebble and pretend it was a jewel. He would peer at it and be disappointed when he finally realized she had been teasing him. She would call his name and dart away – he could never catch her. She pestered this old fish, not thinking of the hurt she was causing.

One day, Mischief was exploring some tall cliffs some way from the castle. (There are lots of tall cliffs under the sea.) She swam close to tickle a starfish and reached out to dangle a piece of seaweed close to a sea urchin's mouth (it would have tasted horrible). It wasn't very nice of her, was it?

As she reached in towards the sea urchin, a huge chunk of rock came away from the cliff and fell right on her tail. Her tail was trapped. She pulled and heaved – but it was no good. She couldn't move it. She was so frightened. How would she ever get home to the castle and back to her sisters? She pulled and pulled until she was exhausted.

As it happened, Grouper was not too far away. He had come to this place for a little peace and quiet. He was not too happy when he heard Mischief calling out. At first, he thought she was just teasing him again and swam slowly on. Mischief watched him go – she was desperate. She called out again.

Grouper was a little worried – she had sounded upset. He decided to go back and see if she was in trouble.

He went back slowly until he was near enough for his old eyes to see that Mischief was stuck and very upset. He knew he wasn't strong enough to lift the rock. He thought for a moment and realized that they were near the den of Ollie, the octopus. Ollie would be strong enough – if he could be persuaded to help.

Groper hurried to the cave in the cliff where Ollie was asleep. Grouper tugged one of Ollie's arms – "We need your help," and he told Ollie about the Mischief and the rock.

At first, Ollie was reluctant to help Mischief – she had played tricks on him. But at last, Grouper persuaded him to lend an arm; actually, eight arms. They hurried back to Mischief, and Ollie grabbed hold of the rock with his strong arms. He gave a mighty tug. The rock moved and fell – further into the depths of the Ocean. Mischief was free.

But her tail was very sore, and she could only swim very slowly. She was a long way from home. Grouper said, "Don't worry, I will stay with you until you are safe back at the castle."

As they made their slow way back, the sea creatures greeted Grouper as an old friend. He had always been kind to them, and they liked him. Even the wicked shark, who roamed the seas frightening many of the smaller fish, smiled to see Grouper and kept them company for a while. No one would dare to hurt them while they were with the killer shark.

The two travelers finally reached the castle garden. Mischief's sisters were looking for her, and they were beginning to get worried. The shark swam away to avoid frightening them more. Grouper left her and swam slowly away. He was happy that he was able to help her, but now he was very tired. He needed to rest.

The sisters were happy to see Mischief was a safe home.

"You were very lucky to have Grouper there to help you," said Merci.

"Ollie must be very strong – but he might not have helped you if Grouper hadn't asked him," said Merry.

"Did you see any pretty shells there?" asked Michelle.

"I think Grouper was very kind," said Me.

Mischief went to bed. Her tail was still very sore, and she wasn't going swimming for a while, but she got bored lying in bed. Her sisters didn't want to hang about for very long, so there was no one to talk to for hours and hours.

After a day or so, Grouper came to see her. He was a bit shy as she had teased him so much, but he was a kind old fish. Mischief was very glad to see him. They chatted for a while, and Grouper brought in some board games to play. He told her magical tales of long ago.

When Mischief was better and could swim again, she visited Grouper. She found that the old fish needed a little help. He couldn't find the best food anymore and had been living on any old scraps he could find. Mischief knew where all the best food was and decided she would make sure Grouper had plenty in the future.

But more than food, Grouper needed company. Mischief remembered how lonely she had felt when she was stuck in bed. She liked seeing him. His stories entranced her, and he was so gentle and kind. She often went to see him. She visited him not just because she felt she ought to but also because he made her feel good. When she was kind to him, she felt a sense of warmth inside herself.

She decided to experiment. She would find a kind deed to do every day to some unsuspecting soul and see how that felt.

She found that it felt good, very good, deep inside her. After a while, she noticed that other sea creatures were more friendly. They no longer tried to avoid her and her tricks. They liked the new Mischief.

Mischief still liked to tell terrible jokes – but they never hurt anyone. She still got into mischief occasionally, but Mischief had learned to be kind, and she had never been happier.

And Grouper? He lived for many more years, comfortable and pampered – as he deserved.

Merry Learns to Control Her Temper

Far, far away, under the deep blue sea, there is a castle in the deepest depths of the Ocean. In the castle live five mermaids, and their names are Merci, Mischief, and Merry, Michelle, and Me.

Of coral is the castle made; the windows are of pearly oyster shells. The roof is of the golden treasure sank beneath the waves. Round the castle is a garden, with fronds of seaweed waving gently in the current. Bright fish of many colors dart amongst the seaweed, like birds amongst our trees. The sandy bottom blooms with sea urchins, starfish, and many other beautiful sea creatures and flowers. The garden is bright with color, reds, and yellows, deep greens and rusty browns all set off against the blue of the moving water.

All the little mermaids had long, flowing hair and jeweled combs. All the little mermaids had twisty, twitchy tails. And sometimes, but not very often, all the little mermaids would lose their tempers. But it was Merry who lost it most of all.

Merry was the happiest and kindest little mermaid you can imagine. But sometimes, she just lost her temper - and then she was *horrid.*

One day she seemed to be in a terrible mood from the moment she woke up.

When Michelle borrowed her pearl necklace without asking (which she should not have done), Merry went red in the face and thrashed her tail from side to side. She looked to be a very cross little mermaid.

When Merci was singing when Merry was trying to listen to the sound a conch shell makes when you hold it close to your ear, Merry threw the conch shell down and stalked off in a huff.

And when Mischief played a small joke on her, she turned around and batted Mischief with her tail.

I had been watching all this with big round eyes; I wouldn't dare upset Merry.

Merry seemed to be trying to cause as much trouble as she could. But every time she lost her temper, she felt bad inside. She decided to go for a long swim, hoping she would feel better. I tagged along behind, feeling that Merry was unhappy and might need company.

Now, it so happened that Dolly the dolphin was going to watch the sailors in a big sailing vessel a long, long way off. Dolly was a bit late starting out, and the other dolphins were ahead of her, so she wanted to swim quickly to catchup to them.

Merry decided she would like a ride - she wanted to see the sailing ship, but it was too far for her to swim there all by herself, so she asked Dolly for a ride.

Dolly said, "No! I'm in a hurry."

Merry said, "I'm not very big; take me with you."

"No," said Dolly.

And Dolly swam away.

Merry was furious, and she caught hold of Dolly's flipper and refused to let go.

"Let go," said Dolly. She was getting cross, too.

"NO!" shouted the mermaid. "Take me. Take me. Take me."

"No, no, no. I won't take you!"

"I won't let go," shouted the mermaid. "Take me, take me, take me."

"No, no, no. I won't take you!"

"Take me, take me, take me."

"No, no, no. I won't take you!"

"Take me, take me, take me."

"No, no, no. I won't take you!"

I had been watching this with big round eyes. Suddenly, Dolly had an idea.

She darted in front of Dolly and shouted – yes - she shouted, "AND I LIKE BAKED BEANS ON MONDAY!"

Merry looked at her – "WHAT did you say?"

Dolly stared at her - "What did you SAY?"

Merry let go of Dolly's fin. Suddenly she began to giggle.

That was sooooo ridiculous!

Dolly swam away, grinning. What an odd little mermaid Merry was!

A few days later, Merry was having another bad day. This time, she was determined to borrow a pretty necklace from Michelle, who had a lovely collection. But Michelle wanted to wear it herself that day and said. "No, not today."

"I want it NOW!" cried Merry.

You can't have it now – not ever." Michelle was getting crosser and crosser

"NOW. NOW. I want it NOW," screamed Merry.

"NO. NO. YOU can't have it."

"I want it.'

"You can't have it."

"I want it."

"You can't have it."

"I want it."

"You can't have it."

"AND I LIKE BAKED BEANS ON MONDAY," shouted Merry.

Michelle gawked at her. WHAT did she say?

"What did you say? You don't even LIKE baked beans."

Merry started to laugh. Then she said, quite politely, "Please, may I borrow your necklace today?"

Michelle was so surprised that she stopped and thought for a moment. She wanted to wear that one herself, but perhaps Merry would like to choose a different necklace. The sapphire one would suit her very well.

"Not that one. Sorry, but if you would like to borrow either the small conch shell necklace or the one with a sapphire, you are welcome."

Merry was pleased. She had always liked the sapphire necklace.

She was thoughtful, too. Why had Michelle suddenly agreed to lend her one of her best necklaces? Why had she changed her mind?

Was it because I surprised her? Or was it because I asked politely? Or was it both?

She was soon to put it to the test.

She was playing with Ollie the Octopus - a form of cat's cradle with long lengths of seaweed. In the game, you must try to make the seaweed look like boats, or caves – or cradles. It's called "cat's cradle" because, as you know, when anyone knits and a cat is around, the cat plays with the wool. It chases it around, and often the wool unwinds and ends up in terrible tangles.

Well, this time, it was Ollie's ARMS that were getting tangled up. After all, if you have eight arms, it can be quite difficult to remember where each of them is. He was getting mixed up with the seaweed. But Merry had spent a long time trying to make the cat's cradle look like a seahorse - and Ollie was messing about and spoiling it. Merry felt her temper beginning to rise. But this time she thought – "DO I like baked beans on Monday? Or should I be nice and help Ollie untangle himself, even if it spoils my seahorse?

The thought of baked beans made her giggle.

"Why are you giggling?" asked Ollie. He was getting upset with his arms, all twisted and tangled. His breath was coming in rapid gasps. His little heart was pumping madly.

"Never mind," replied Merry. "Let's sort out your arms!"

Gently she unraveled the seaweed. Her seahorse came to pieces, but Ollie's arms straightened out. Soon he was smiling again. He reached out with his arms and felt them strong and then soften as he drew them in. His breathing slowed down to its normal slow rate. His heart beat strongly and steadily again.

And Merry? She had found that laugher was a great way not to lose your temper. She felt light and happy as she watched the little octopus relax.

Merry relaxed with him. She matched her breathing to his, slow and deep. She reached out gently to stroke the seaweed into patterns and shapes. How nice to know that unexpected things can change bad words to funny words. And being polite often made the other person be kind to you. Losing your temper just felt bad – and it didn't help you get what you wanted.

Michelle Shares Her Treasures

Far, far away, under the deep blue sea, there is a castle in the deepest depths of the Ocean. In the castle live five mermaids, and their names are Merci, Mischief, and Merry, Michelle, and Me.

Of coral is the castle made; the windows are of pearly oyster shells. The roof is of the golden treasure sank beneath the waves. Round the castle is a garden, with fronds of seaweed waving gently in the current. Bright fish of many colors dart amongst the seaweed, like birds amongst our trees. The sandy bottom blooms with sea urchins, starfish, and many other beautiful sea creatures and flowers. The garden is bright with color, reds, and yellows, deep greens and rusty browns all set off against the blue of the moving water.

All the little mermaids had long, flowing hair and jeweled combs. All the little mermaids had twisty, twitchy tails. They all liked pretty things. But the mermaid who loved pretty things the most was Michelle.

Michelle collected treasures she would hoard in her room. She collected odd-shaped pieces of seaweed - until they began to smell. She collected pretty stones. She liked the smooth ones best, but sometimes there was one with a curly, cracked, and interesting shape.

Most of all, Michelle collected shells. As you can imagine, there were lots and lots of shells lying on the seafloor. And there were lots and lots of shells in Michelle's room in the castle. There were so many shells in her room that you could hardly open the door - and if you did, you had to be very, very careful not to tread on any.

When the little mermaids went exploring the beautiful watery world, Michelle would go ahead, grabbing the best shells for herself. She could be quite selfish when she wanted something she thought was pretty.

One day, the five little mermaids were swimming around a coral reef. They saw the bright little fishes darting in and out of the crevices. They saw the sea urchins waving their tendrils in the gentle current. And then Michell saw a fine, smooth shell. She went to pick it up.

As she did, two eyes stared back at her from inside the shell.

"This shell is in use," said the crab who lived there.

"Sorry," said Michelle. She swam on - even Michelle would not disturb a little hermit crab in its home.

But she did manage to find a striped conch shell and a shiny oyster shell. She carried them back to her room. She opened the door - and looked inside. So much treasure - but it didn't look very bright or sparkly heaped up in her room. She felt a little disappointed. Perhaps she should go and look for something brighter and more sparkly?

The very next day, Michelle set off. She went by herself this time as the other little mermaids were happy just to play in the castle garden, enjoying all the lovely things there - the fronds of seaweed, the starfish on the sandy bottom, the bright little fishes are darting amongst the rocks and weeds.

Michelle set off on her lonely journey. She swam along the rocky cliffs. She swam around the coral reef. She swam till she was tired and aching all over. She found nothing new, nothing special, nothing she really wanted.

Eventually, Michelle turned back. She was beginning to think that perhaps all the treasures she wanted was already back at the castle.

Going back into her room she looked around. It all seemed dull. It didn't make her feel happy. What was she to do?

Michelle decided there and then that she didn't want - and she didn't need - any of the jumble of stuff she had collected and hoarded. What use was it to her crammed up in her room? No one could see it. No one could feel it. No one knew it was there. Even she didn't' know what she had.

She started to clear the room, carrying armfuls of shells and stones and seaweeds out into the castle garden. The things looked much nicer out there. The other little mermaids came to see what she was up to.

"Whatever are you doing?" asked Merci. "Oh, look there is a beautiful conch shell, can we see if it makes a good sound when I blow it." She blew, and the conch shell gave out a deep sound like a giant horn.

"You can have it if you like," said Michelle.

Merci was very pleased. She had always wanted a big conch shell to make music with.

"You have an awful lot of stones," said Mischief. "Can we make a rockery in the garden with them?" asked Merry.

"Oh, yes," said Michelle. "They will look so interesting there – and we can all see them there."

I helped Michell carry out the shells. "What shall we do with these?" she asked.

They decided to edge the garden pathways with pretty shells. Soon most of Michelle's treasures were decorating the garden where they could all see them, or special pieces had been given away.

Michelle looked at the small pile left. She picked out one dark, rounded stone and stroked its cool, smooth surface. She chose a few shells to make into a necklace, and that was all. The rest of her old treasures drifted away, free for anyone to look at, to admire, to enjoy.

Michelle went back to her room that night to sleep. She opened the door easily without having to push against "treasures." There was plenty of space to move across the room. There was no smell of old seaweed.

Michell felt good inside. She had given her treasure away. She had found that giving was better than hoarding. She knew that she could find new shells and stones when she wanted to, but that sharing them made her feel all warm inside.

Her real treasure was inside herself! She drifted on the gentle movement of the sea surrounding her. Her hands trailed in the ocean around her. Her eyes closed, the sea rocked her softly and smoothly... gently and smoothly...gently ...and smoothly...

Softly she entered dreamland. She smiled in her sleep...gently swaying in the deep warm water...softly smiling...softly smiling in her sleep.

I am Happy to be Me

Far, far away, under the deep blue sea, there is a castle in the deepest depths of the Ocean. In the castle live five mermaids, and their names are Merci, Mischief, and Merry, Michelle, and Me.

Of coral is the castle made; the windows are of pearly oyster shells. The roof is of the golden treasure sank beneath the waves. Round the castle is a garden, with fronds of seaweed waving gently in the current. Bright fish of many colors dart amongst the seaweed, like birds amongst our trees. The sandy bottom blooms with sea urchins, starfish, and many other beautiful sea creatures and flowers. The garden is bright with color, reds, and yellows, deep greens and rusty browns all set off against the blue of the moving water.

All the little mermaids had long, flowing hair and jeweled combs. All the little mermaids had twisty, twitchy tails. But the smallest little mermaid was Me. And sometimes she wished she was a little bit bigger, like her sisters.

One day when the sun was making dappled patterns on the sandy bottom of the sea, the five little mermaids went exploring. They swam gracefully out of the castle garden and over the shelly banks where the sea urchins waved their fronds in the warm water. They swam slowly among the twisty seaweed, stopping every now and then as Michelle found another shell.

She would stroke the shell's surface – sometimes rough, but often smooth and hard. Some were shiny, others were dull, and many were encrusted with smaller shells. They would wonder who lived in the shells. Sometimes they saw a hermit crab that had made a home for himself in an empty shell. Once, they noticed a tiny octopus, pulling in his arms as they passed.

They came to the cliff where Mischief had been trapped by the falling rock, and they kept well away. But further along, they thought they heard a faint cry. Merci heard it first – a long, wailing sound. They all stopped and listened. It seemed to be coming from inside the rock. It seemed to be calling for help.

Merci called out, and a faint answer came floating back. "Help me. Help me."

They looked at the cliffs in front of them. How could the sound be coming from there? Then Merry saw a tiny hole in the rocks, half-covered by seaweed.

"I think the sound is coming from there," she said. And she crept closer. Putting her ear to the crack, she nodded. "Yes – but it's far too small for me to go through."

Mischief was usually bolder than her sisters, but this time she remembered how frightened she had been when she was trapped.

The mermaids looked at one another. Then Me said, "I think I could squeeze through."

She took off her coral necklace and her conch shell bracelets, lest they get caught in the rough rock. Then she took a big breath. She was scared!

She dived through the tiny crack – even for Me, it was a squeeze. Me was nervous. She was breathing quickly, her heart was dashing away, and she had a dozen little fish playing her tummy.

She wriggled her way through a narrow twisty passageway. The pathway opened out, and she found herself in an underwater cavern. It was lit by glowing fish with phosphorescent bodies and bright, flashy tails.

Around the walls were sea flowers of many colors. There were reds, blues, and greens, sparkling with silver and gold. There were stones of many colors on the floor– some as red as rubies, some like pale green emeralds, and some blue, flashing sapphires. There were dark opals and translucent diamonds – it was a treasure cave.

And all around were hanging crystal stalactites, adorned with wispy fronds of strange sea plants. It was very still in the cave. Nothing was moving. It was a magical place.

And there, shivering in a corner, was an odd-looking creature. It seemed to be a mouth – with huge, sharp teeth. It was quiet now and watched Me with big, blue eyes.

"Who are you?" asked Me.

"I'm a fangtooth fish," replied the strange creature. "And I can't find my way out."

Me looked around. Was she lost too? Where was the entrance to the tunnel she had come in? She couldn't see it anywhere.

"Don't worry," she said bravely. "We'll find the way out."

The fish wasn't very big, but it had terrible teeth. She really didn't want to get too close. She really didn't. But he looked so afraid, she went over to him and gently stroked his tail.

Turning, she gazed over the cave, and then she noticed one of the seaweed branches was drifting about a little. "That must be where the exit is," thought Me.

"Follow me, Fangtooth," she cried, and set off towards the exit. It was very narrow, and she had to twist and turn her little body to pass through the passageway. She twisted this way and that, she bent her tail up and straightened it. She breathed in and then let her breathe out, her chest getting smaller. And all the time she talked to Fangtooth, encouraging him to follow her.

At last, the passageway ended, and they found themselves back in the open ocean.

Fangtooth thanked her and disappeared down into the depths of the sea where he belonged. He was a very lucky little fish.

The mermaids hugged Me and said how brave she was. As they swam slowly back to the castle, she told them about the magical cave. They all agreed that the treasure was best left alone – they had treasure enough in the free seas around them, in their own castle garden – and the love they had for each other.

Me was feeling relaxed and happy. She was proud that she had rescued the little fangtooth fish. She was proud of the way she had gone into a narrow, fearful passage without knowing what she would find. As she swam lazily back home, she felt warm and content.

Reaching the castle, she lay down to rest. "It's lucky I am so small," she thought.

Her tail flopped down, her breaths came slow, her eyelids dropped, and soon the little mermaid was fast asleep. She dreamed of treasure never to be touched. She dreamed of all the good things she had and smiled in her sleep.

Chapter 4: The Tales of Doughnut, the Dancing Dinosaur

Doughnut Dresses Up

One morning, Doughnut was in the bedroom watching Mommy Dino getting ready to go out to work. First, she put on some lipstick, then she outlined her eyes and added a little blusher. Doughnut thought she looked fabulous. Then she reached for a crisp white blouse and a sleek black skirt. Finally, she thrust her (rather large) feet into (rather large) shoes with very high heels. Doughnut thought she looked amazing.

Mommy Dino tottered into the kitchen to make breakfast. She plonked a dish of "Little Dino" cereal in front of Doughnut. (How boring!) She put the coffee on and made herself some toast.

Doughnut spilled a little milk on the floor (accidentally-on-purpose). He wanted a grown-up breakfast, just like mommy. He wanted toast with lots and lots of strawberry jam. But mommy was in a hurry.

As she went to the cupboard to get herself some jam, she slipped in the milk – and that made her cross. Then she dropped a tiny little bit of bright red jam onto her white blouse – and that made her crosser. She rushed back into the bedroom and came back, wearing a red blouse.

"How sensible," though Doughnut. "Now, even if she does spill jam, it won't show."

Doughnut sat very still.

"Oh! I'm so late," cried mommy. She gave Doughnut a quick kiss and rushed out – saying, "Clear up, will you," – and she didn't even say please!

Doughnut felt sad. Work was important, he knew, but he felt that he was not.

Maybe if he looked like mommy, then mommy would notice him more, and he would feel more special.

"I'll put on a show for her when she comes back," Doughnut thought. "I'll dress up and dance; then, mommy will notice me and be pleased."

Doughnut went back into the bedroom. The wardrobe door was wide open.

First, Doughnut tried on a skirt. It was far too big for him. He kept tripping over it. Soon there was a big tear in the skirt - but when he twirled around, the skirt opened out and whirled around with him.

Mommy Dino had lots and lots of hats. She kept them on top of the wardrobe. Doughnut reached up - but he was too small to reach them. He jumped up - but still, they were too high up. Then he took a mighty dancers leap - and they all came tumbling down.

There was a big purple hat, a tiny red hat with cherries bobbing up and down on it. There was a ginormous blue hat with lots of feathers - that was the one for Doughnut.

As he danced, the feathers slowly came off the hat and floated down - all over the bedroom.

Time for some makeup! He needed lots of it. First, a bright slash of scarlet lipstick - somehow, went all over his face - but he thought it looked cool. Then, mascara - his big dark eyes looked enormous, with great black rings round them. Then, the blusher - there was hardly any room left on his face - so he piled it on top of the red lipstick and the black mascara.

He looked at himself in the mirror. Somehow, it didn't look quite right. Doughnut was getting upset. He noticed the tear in the skirt. He looked at the feathers all over the floor. Somehow, he wasn't sure anymore. Maybe mommy would be cross, and he so much wanted to please her.

Bang - the front door. Mommy was home. Oh, dear.

Mommy came to the bedroom door. She gasped!

And then she threw back her head and laughed. She laughed till the tears ran down her cheeks. Her mascara smudged. Doughnut gave a little giggle - and then he gave a little laugh. Then he laughed and laughed till the tears ran down his face. She came into the room very gently and gave Doughnut a hug - a big, squishy hug.

"I wanted you to like me," said Doughnut, "I was going to dance for you. I wanted to be just like you."

Mommy said, "I love you just the way you are. We had better clean up all this, and then you can dance for me – my own little Doughnut."

So, the two of them swept up the feathers with big sweeping movements.

They wiped down the cupboards, up and down and round and round.

They washed the floor, squishy-squashy, squishy-squashy, and soon the bedroom looked tidy. It smelt lovely and clean.

"We make a great team," said his mommy.

After tea, mommy sat down to mend the torn skirt. As she sat there, her little Doughnut danced for her. He stretched up his arms; he waggled his fingers. He reached down with his feet and wriggled his Doughnut toes. Then he let his muscles relax and go all soft and gooey.

Mommy reached out for him and cuddled him on her knee. He was tired after such an exciting day. He felt warm, and every part of him felt soft and heavy: his toes felt soft and heavy, his feet felt soft and heavy, his legs felt soft and floppy, his body felt soft and sleepy – he heard his mommy murmuring to him – "I love you just the way you are" as his neck felt soft and warm and his face felt soft...and his eyelids felt heavy... and heavier...

Soon his eyes closed, and little Doughnut was fast asleep. He knew he was fine – just the way he was.

Doughnut, the Dinosaur, Goes to School

It was Doughnut's first day at school. He was excited – and a little bit nervous, too.

As a treat, Mommy made his toast with lots of strawberry jam. But Doughnut wasn't hungry. His tummy felt like a bar of iron inside him. He had a smart new shirt and shorts (with four legs since this little dinosaur had four legs). And he had new shoes – they squeaked as he walked, and he wasn't sure he liked that.

Mommy and Doughnut set off along the lane to school. It seemed a long way, and mommy tried to hurry him along, and Doughnut wanted to lag. Suddenly, mommy fell over – she had been going too fast. She had cut her knee, and it was bleeding. What was Doughnut to do?

There was a little cottage beside the path. Doughnut decided they need help, so he knocked on the door. A kind lady came out and saw that mommy needed a bandage. She invited them in, washed the wound, and put on a big plaster. Mommy felt a lot better after that. She thanked the kind lady, and they carried on down the lane to school. But she didn't rush anymore!

As they were walking along, the kind lady overtook them on her bicycle and waved. Doughnut noticed she was wearing a funny little hat with a nest on top – and a bird in the nest. He wanted to have a closer look; fancy – a bird in a nest on a hat! But the lady rode past without stopping.

At last, Doughnut and his mommy arrived at the school door. And guess who was there to greet them. The kind lady with the funny hat – except she wasn't wearing the hat anymore. Doughnut said goodbye to mommy and went inside the classroom.

It looked very big, and there were lots of other little dinosaurs making such a noise! Doughnut saw a big table with thick green and red cover, which went right down to the floor, all the way around. Doughnut eyed it – it would make a nice den, he thought. He crept under the table and hid. He felt a bit safer there, out of the way. It was dark under the table, and the floor was hard – but Doughnut was glad to be away from the other shouting dinosaurs.

After a while, it grew quiet. Doughnut peeped through a crack in the tablecloth. All the little dinosaurs were sitting in a circle with the kind lady in the center. They started to sing. It was a song he had bever heard before – and it made no sense to him. "ABCDEFG-HIJKLMNOP-QRSTUV-WXY and Z." Do you know that song?

Doughnut liked to sing, and he wanted to join in – perhaps tomorrow?

Doughnut watched with big eyes – it was all so strange. He saw the little dinosaurs stand up and play a game – "Simon Says." Maybe you know that game?

"Simon says – 'Put your front feet in the air'" – and all at the little dinosaurs put up their hands (or front feet).

"Simon says – 'Shake your feet'" – and all the little dinosaurs shook their feet.

"Simon says – "Wiggle your tummy'" – and all the little dinosaurs wiggled their tummies – that made Doughnut giggle.

"Open your mouths wide," – but only one little dinosaur opened his mouth. He laughed and went to sit and watch while the others continued to play.

After a while, Doughnut felt a small bit of air – and the dinosaur who had opened his mouth slid under the table to join him. Soon, one by one, the other little dinosaurs joined them under the table! It began to get quite crowded. Then Doughnut heard a whistle blow, and all the little dinosaurs vanished. It was playtime. Doughnut was tired after all the excitement and decided to have a little nap in the dark under the table.

He stretched out – but the floor was hard. He tossed and turned, but he could not get comfortable. He thought perhaps he would be very brave and go out to see what everyone was doing. He peeped out, blinking in the bright light.

As he crept out, he saw the teacher struggling to lift a large shiny blue box onto the table. It seemed to be too heavy for her, and her face was going redder and redder. Some of the other little dinosaurs were trying to help – but they were not strong enough either. Doughnut knew he was strong. All that dancing had made his muscles very strong – and for a little dinosaur, he was stronger than anyone would think. After all, a dancing dinosaur must be able to lift another dinosaur - and make it look easy.

So, he knew he had to help. Doughnut left the shelter of the table and went over to the struggling crowd. He tucked himself under the others, seized hold of the bottom of the shiny blue box. He took a big breath, and holding his breath, he tensed all his muscles and heaved. The box shot up onto the table.

Then he retreated under the table again as fast as he could.

"How did that happen?" demanded the teacher. "One minute, we couldn't lift the box, and then it seemed to lift up all by itself."

"I think there is a dinosaur under the table," said one little dinosaur. "He helped."

Now, the teacher knew that Doughnut was hiding. Perhaps it was time to invite him out? She opened the tablecloth a little and asked him whether he would like to show them how strong he was. The next lesson was a dancing lesson - and none of the boy dinos had a clue how to dance. Some of them even though it was sissy - not the thing for a boy dino to do.

Doughnut came out of hiding. The teacher put some music on. Doughnut and the girl dinos started to dance. When Doughnut was dancing, he would forget everything else - he moved to the music and felt he was gliding on air. The boys watched. Some of the girls found that a Doughnut could help them twirl and skirl, and soon all the girls were whirling around the floor.

They were moving faster and faster; the music was louder and louder. Soon all the little dinos were dancing. Then Doughnut lifted one of the girls- high and higher. With care, he set her down. He felt strong and happy. Everyone clapped.

Now it was time to cool down. Doughnut knew this was important, or his muscles would ache the next day. He showed them how to cool down the proper way.

"Stretch your whole body up," he said. "Then, stretch your legs and feet. Front legs and back legs. Move your neck slowly. Looking from side to side - up and down. Be very gentle and slow."

"Then reach up one last time with a big stretch - and breathe in - all the way. Then breathe out slowly."

"Take another big breath - in and out - and you are done."

Doughnut was surprised to find that he had come out of hiding. He was surprised to find that the other little dinosaurs were interested in him. He was surprised when the bell went for the end of the school day.

Mommy was at the door to meet him. Doughnut told her all about his first day at school.

Mommy said, "Doughnut when you think about other people, you forget to be nervous yourself. I am so proud of you for helping the teacher – and I am proud that you were brave enough to show the others that dancing makes you fit and strong – and isn't just for the girls!"

Doughnut Visits His Grandmother

Doughnut would visit his grandmother, who lived in a little cottage at the end of her village. Doughnut and his mommy had to catch a train to visit her – it meant they would be away for a whole day.

Mommy had baked some cookies for grandma, and Doughnut picked some colorful blue and yellow flowers. He made them into a bunch of sweet-smelling flowers. He wrapped a lacy white doily round them. They did look pretty.

On the way to the station to catch the train, Doughnut was dancing along the sidewalk as he usually did; he never seemed to walk in a straight line anywhere! He caught his shoe in a crack, and the shoe came off. He tried to pull it out – but it was stuck – it just wouldn't come out. So, his mommy tried. She couldn't pull it out either.

A police car was passing – it stopped. A big, smiley policeman climbed out.

"What are you doing to the sidewalk?" he asked.

"My little dinosaur has caught his shoe in the crack, and we can't pull it out," replied his mommy.

"Let me have a go," said the policeman.

He bent down and seized hold of the shoe – and pulled. He pulled some more, and his face started to go red with the effort. At last, with a mighty heave, the shoe came free – and the policeman sat down!

He started to laugh. Mommy gave him a hand to get up, and then she giggled. Doughnut giggled, and then he started to laugh - and he couldn't stop. Every time he looked up at the big policeman, he started to giggle again.

His mommy was embarrassed - "It wasn't that funny," she said. "Say 'thank you' to the kind policeman."

Doughnut managed to splutter a thank you - he really was very grateful.

"Oh, dear," cried his mom, "we are going to miss the train."

Sure enough, in the distance, they could hear the train wheezing along.

"Quick, jump into my car," the policeman cried.

He drove them to the station very fast. The police siren was blaring out. The policeman jumped out with them and rushed to the platform. Mommy bought the tickets, and the policeman held up the train, so they just managed to climb aboard before it wheezed out of the station. Doughnut waved and waved at the kind policeman.

They sank back into their seats. Every now and then, Doughnut gave a little giggle. His mommy rolled her eyes!

When they arrived at the country station, Doughnut's grandma was waiting to meet them. She had a very old car with stickers all over it - you could hardly see that it was painted green. It smelled of old leather and sticky buns. (Grandma was a great cook.)

She was very old. Her hair was a lovely white and shiny color. Her eyes were blue - a soft grey-blue. But guess what she was wearing?

She had on a bright purple skirt and an orange blouse with green splotches on it. She said she had made it herself. On her head was a green feather - just one green feather. "I didn't want to overdo it," she said, as Doughnut admired her feather. Her necklaces and bracelets jangled as she talked - there were gold bracelets, silver ones, and huge beads round her neck. Grandma loved dressing up!

Doughnut thought she looked great!

Once in the cottage, Doughnut gave grandma the flowers he had picked. She was very pleased and immediately put them in a vase of water. Flowers can get very thirsty. Then grandma made some sandwiches and sent Doughnut out to play. But he soon got tired of the garden – it was full of weeds, and there was no swing, no trampoline. "In fact," he thought, "there is nothing to do."

He went back inside. The grown-up dinosaurs were chatting away and ignored him.

Doughnut went back outside. He opened the door of the shed and saw a spade. Now, Doughnut was strong, and he was a nice little dinosaur. He dragged out the spade and dug up the whole garden to rid it of weeds. The trouble was, he wasn't too sure which were weeds and which were not.

However, that didn't stop him. He set off to work.

He pushed down the spade. He put his foot on it and pushed down some more; the spade sank into the earth; he gave it a twist and pulled it out. He shook off the soil clinging to the roots of the plants.

It was lucky that Grandma and mommy came out and look at the garden, just as Doughnut was about to take another shovel full of "weeds."

"Oh!" cried Grandma.

"Oh, dear!" cried mommy.

Grandma thought for a moment; she could see that Doughnut was upset.

"Would you like a little space just for you?" she asked. "We can buy some flowers, and you can plant them, and you can come and look after them when you are here."

Doughnut thought that would be a great idea. The whole garden was far too big for a little dinosaur.

His grandma helped him mark off a sunny corner in the garden,

"This is all yours," she said.

Doughnut worked hard. He collected ginormous stones to make a border. He dug out most of the weeds. His grandma found some plants among all the weeds (they were real flowers.) They wanted to be free of the weeds and have room to grow – up into the sunshine.

All too soon, it was time to catch the train home. They climbed into grandma's old car – it seemed to be even older than grandma.

As they said goodbye, grandma gave Doughnut the green feather from her hair. She tickled his cheek as she said, "Thank you for all your hard work in the garden, your corner looks so pretty. This will remind you of your special place at my home."

Doughnut and his mommy boarded the train and sat down. Doughnut stroked his cheek with the green feather; it felt soft and tickly. He felt so sleepy. The train went chug, chug, chug. He cuddled up under his warm coat. The train went chug, chug, chug.

Doughnut gave a deep sigh. The train went chug, chug, chug. Doughnut relaxed; he closed his eyes. The train went chug, chug, chug. Chug...chug...and soon the little dinosaur was fast asleep.

Doughnut Goes to the Seaside

Doughnut and his family were going to the seaside.

"But I haven't got anything to wear!" cried Doughnut.

"All you need are some bathing trunks," said daddy. "Mommy can take you shopping to buy some."

So, mommy and Doughnut set off to the shop. They were the first customers to arrive. Doughnut was excited.

The shop was full of all the things you need for a day out to the seaside. There were buckets and spades and tiny flags. They bought a blue bucket and a yellow spade.

"Do you think the blue bucket is big enough? asked Doughnut. I want to build a great big sandcastle.

"Maybe not, said mommy dino. "We'll get a green one as well - it's big. Perhaps you will need a fork as well as the spade?"

So, they put the blue bucket, and the green bucket, the yellow spade, and the fork into the shopping cart. Doughnut added a few flags while mommy wasn't looking.

There were beach towels in all the colors you can think of. Mommy thought some beach towels would be a good idea. She bought a pretty one with a flowery pattern for herself, she bought a bright blue one for daddy, But Doughnut couldn't decide – red with trains on it or the yellow one with stars? Mommy ended up buying both – after all, he was a good little dinosaur.

So now they had the blue bucket and the green bucket, the yellow spade and the fork, a few flags and a pretty flowery towel, a bright blue towel and a red towel with trains on it and a yellow towel with stars. The cart was getting rather full.

Then they saw a fold-up chair ."We better have two of those," said mommy. "And a beach umbrella to keep off the sun." Doughnut had to carry that as the shopping cart was too full. He opened it up and danced around with it till mommy told him, "Behave!"

Finally, Mommy put in a blow-up Lilo for Doughnut to lie on. It's lucky dinosaurs are strong to carry all those things!

When they arrived home, they showed daddy all the good things they had bought for the day beside the sea. They showed him the blue bucket, the green bucket, the yellow spade and the fork, a few flags and a pretty flowery towel, a bright blue towel and a red towel with trains on it and a yellow towel stars. They showed him the fold-up chairs and the parasol. And the Lilo.

Daddy dino scratched his head.

"You have been busy," he said, " but what are you going to wear?"

Oh dear, they had forgotten to buy the one thing they had gone into the shop to buy – the swimming trunks.

"Never mind," said daddy. "Come with me now, and we will buy the swimming trunks for you."

They got back with a pair of swimming trunks for Doughnut – and nothing else at all.

Early the next day, they set off for the beach in daddy's car. Doughnut was a bit squashed in the back there was so much stuff to cram in. There was the blue bucket and the green bucket, the yellow spade and the fork, a few flags and a pretty flowery towel, a bright blue towel and a red towel with trains on it and a yellow towel with stars.

There were the fold-up chairs and the parasol. And the Lilo. And a big basket of picnic food – dinosaurs like their food!

Doughnut saved space by wearing his new swimming trunks.

They soon arrived at the beach and parked the car. Mommy went ahead onto the beach to find a nice place to stay for the day. Then daddy and Doughnut joined her with all the gear.

Doughnut felt the sand, hot and prickly on his feet as he walked across to mommy. He was hot. Carrying all the things they had was hard work. Doughnut was thirsty; his tongue was sticking to the roof of his mouth. It felt a bit like the sand – hot and very dry. He laid out his red towel with trains on it and collapsed in a heap. Mommy gave him a huge bottle of orange juice, and the whole family settled under the parasol.

It wasn't long before Doughnut began to look around. He got up – time to make that sandcastle. Doughnut stretched and picked up the yellow spade. Then he gave daddy dino the big green bucket, and he took the smaller blue bucket, and they went down, close to the sea, where the sand was damp. They started to build their castle.

First, Doughnut drew a circle in the sand. Then he and daddy filled it with a huge pile of wet sand. Doughnut tried to smooth it down while daddy dino kept adding more and more sand. Soon they had a mountain of sand with a deep moat around it and a high wall. Daddy showed Doughnut how to make sand pies with the bucket. Doughnut loved the squishy sound they made as they came out of the bucket, shaped like little towers. He made sand pies all around the castle walls.

"You need to decorate the castle now," said daddy dino. "I'm going up to sit with mommy – we'll watch you. See what you can find."

Doughnut soon found some green seaweed. He stroked his cheek with it. It felt smooth and wet. It had a salty, seaweedy smell. Then he found some shiny shells. Some were long and thin; some were round and scalloped. But his favorite shells were small yellow ones. He had to get his feet wet to find them.

The sea felt cool and tickled his toes as the little waves danced backward and forwards. The waves made a soft swishy sound as they came in and a soft wheezy sound as they went out.

Looking out to sea, he saw a little girl dino on a Lilo. But she seemed to be a long way out. Most of the dinosaurs were paddling near the edge – very few of them could swim.

The little girl dino was drifting further and further out. There were some bigger waves out there, and the Lilo was dancing up and down, up and down. Doughnut was afraid she could be tipped off. He ran up to his daddy and pointed out the little girl dino on Lilo, way out to sea.

Daddy leaped up. He raced to the lifeguard and pointed to the Lilo. The guard had been helping other dinos to put up their decks-chairs and parasols.

The lifeguard was one of the few dinosaurs who could swim. He dashed into the water and forced his way through the waves. Quickly he reached the little girl dino. He grabbed hold of the Lilo and towed it back to the shore. She held on tight.

The little girl's parents were waiting for her. They had seen the crowd and only then noticed how far she had drifted out to sea. They were very thankful. They thanked the lifeguard – who told them never to let their child climb onto a Lilo in the water without either holding it or watching it all the time. They thanked daddy dino – and they thanked Doughnut.

"Thank you, thank you, thank you," they cried.

Doughnut went back to his castle in the sand. The moat was filling with seawater as the tide was coming in. Small waves lapped the shore. Each one seemed to come a little bit higher up the sand. Doughnut let them play among his toes. The waves felt cool and soft. They dragged at his feet as they went out and pushed against them as they came in.

They were very little waves, and made very little whishing sounds...whish...wash...whish...wash...

Daddy brought the Lilo down to the sea.

"Time for you to rest on the Lilo," he said. "But I will watch you all the time and hold onto this string attached to the Lilo."

Doughnut heaved himself onto the Lilo. He lay back. Daddy was there, watching him. He knew he was safe and that daddy would never let go of the string.

He began to relax. The Lilo bobbed gently up and down...up and down. The sea tasted salty on his lips. The Lilo bobbed gently up and down... up and down... He heard the water rippling along the sides. He heard the little waves pattering on the shore... in and out... in and out...

He gazed up at the blue sky. He saw a small white cloud drifting across - shaped like a dinosaur with wings. He watched it float across the blue, blue sky...

Slowly the little dinosaur drifted off - he was warm, relaxed, safe. Doughnut smiled in his sleep. Daddy watched his little dinosaur and smiled too.

Doughnut, the Dancing Dinosaur, Makes Music

One day, Doughnut was playing with his friends in a nearby field. They were playing hide-and-seek.

Big Dandy Dino was trying to hide behind a tree - but the tree wasn't wide enough. He stuck out behind it, and everyone could see him - except Doughnut, who was looking the wrong way. He was dreaming about a new dance he was making up. But he hadn't got any music that felt right.

He looked for Dandy Dino - in the wrong direction. But, glinting in the long grass, he found something else!

He found a trumpet. A bright, shiny, brass trumpet. It had a little label on it which said:

"He who finds me - and can play 'Twinkle Twinkle Little Star' - all the way through and can keep me. But if you can't play - leave me alone until someone comes along who can play."

Doughnut called the other dinosaurs to see what he had found. Even Dandy came to see. None of the little dinosaurs knew how to play a trumpet. They did think it was very beautiful - shiny brass with little shiny buttons. What were they to do?

They picked up the trumpet, and they all had a turn, trying to play. But all they got were horrible squeals and howling sounds - the trumpet didn't sound happy at all.

"Let's find someone who knows how to play the trumpet," suggested the smallest dinosaur.

"But how will we find him?" asked another.

They went to find Doughnut's mommy and asked her how to find a musical dinosaur, one who could play a trumpet.

"Look for smoke rising to the sky and listen to the sound of the wind. Follow the sound to the smoke, and there you will find the singing dinosaur", said his mommy. "But be very careful to be very polite, you don't want to make the singing dinosaur angry."

So, the little dinosaurs set off to the top of the hill where they could see for miles around. They looked and looked - and just when they thought there was no sign of smoke anywhere and that the musical dinosaur had probably gone early to bed, they saw a tiny swirl of blue smoke - it looked a very long way off.

They all listened, but they were too far away to hear the dinosaur singing. They all walked or ran or fell or rolled down the hill toward the swirl of smoke - but it was hard to see from the lower ground. And then, just peeping above the treetops, they saw the smoke again and set off towards it.

The trees grew thick and close together, and the night was getting dark. The trumpet they carried, in turn, seemed to get heavier and heavier. The little dinosaurs were getting very tired. The smoke had vanished. Just as they thought they couldn't go a step further, they heard a soft, sighing sound though the trees. It sounded so sad.

The little dinosaurs peeped through the branches. They saw a big, droopy dinosaur, lying on his side. He was crying.

The little dinosaurs didn't know what to do. They had never seen a grown-up dinosaur cry. They all looked at Doughnut. He was the one who had found the trumpet. It was his job to sort things out.

Doughnut put the trumpet down and ducked under the low branches and tiptoed to the great big crying dinosaur. He touched him on his shoulder very lightly. There was no response.

Doughnut stood back and tried a small cough. The great big dinosaur looked up. He saw Doughnut.

"Why are you crying?" asked Doughnut, very bravely.

"I have lost my trumpet. I can't make music anymore. There is no one to hear me or to dance to the music."

"Can you play the trumpet?" asked Doughnut.

"Yes, I can play the trumpet," said the great big dinosaur. "But there is no point. I left it for someone else to play, someone who can dance to the music."

"If you will play it, I will dance." Said Doughnut.

The other little dinosaurs came out from behind the bushes. They gave the gleaming trumpet to the great big dinosaur. He was so pleased to see it again.

He started to play a tune.

"Stop," cried Doughnut. "You have to play 'Twinkle, Twinkle, Little Star' first!

The great big dinosaur smiled. He showed all his teeth when he smiled. He had great big teeth.

Doughnut said, "Please?"

The great big dinosaur licked his lips and played 'Twinkle, Twinkle, Little Star.'

Then he played some happy, noisy music, and all the little dinosaurs started to dance. They stretched their little legs. They pointed their little toes. They spun around and whirled and twirled. The music got faster and faster.

Soon they were all out of breath. The collapsed on the ground in a great big laughing heap.

The music died away and became gentle, soft, and slow. The great big dinosaur watched the little ones and played on, a soft whispering sound, the rhythm of a heart beating gently, the sigh of breath breathing softly.

The trees overhead whispered and sighed. The music played on. The little dinosaurs relaxed.

The music stopped. "Time to go home," said the great big dinosaur. "Time for bed."

He led them all the way home, and the little dinosaurs went to their homes, and quite soon, they were all in their own little beds. Outside, the music played on, gentle, and soft, and slow. A soft whispering sound... the rhythm of a heart beating gently...the sigh of breath breathing softly...soon they were all asleep.

All except Doughnut. He was thinking. "If I had kept the trumpet for myself, we would never have met the great big dinosaur. He would still be unhappy. I am glad we found him. I am glad we found his trumpet. He can make music, and I can dance. We can all do something special if we help each other.

With these thoughts, Doughnut smiled and closed his eyes.

Doughnut relaxed, comfortable with his thoughts. Soon he was dreaming... the music calming him... stilling him... lulling him...till he was fast asleep...

Chapter 5: The Adventures of Abblesoc, the Awesome Alien

Abblesoc the Alien Finds a Home

Tom was a happy little boy. He lived with his mommy and daddy in a little house at the edge of a little village. He went to the little village school where he had lots of friends. And now it was bedtime.

Tonight was bath night (ugh). He felt warm and tingly all over, and he did like the smell of the new shampoo.

Every night, before he climbed into bed, Tom would go to the window and look up at the night sky. He wondered whether anyone out there was looking back at him. Tom longed to meet a real, live alien.

And this night – there WAS someone out there!

Abblesoc was afraid. Her spacecraft was exhausted. It had carried her thousands and thousands of miles, weaving through the stars. They had dodged the comets with their fiery tails. They had twisted their way through the asteroids. And they were both tired.

"I can't go much further," groaned the spacecraft. "I need to rest."

Abblesoc knew they had to stop soon. But where? The dark skies seemed almost empty – there was nowhere to land. Then, ahead, she saw a solid, white ball in the sky. It had craters with dark shadows and mountains reaching into space. But it seemed to have a smiling face. Abblesoc knew they must land there.

With a bump, the spacecraft came to rest. It let out a sigh of relief and settled down to rest. Soon the spacecraft was fast asleep. Abblesoc was alone.

She set off to explore. She needed water. She needed food. She needed shelter.

But there was no one to welcome her; no food, no water, no shelter - nothing. She was quite alone. She was shivering with cold and trembling with fear.

The ground was dry and bare. Dusty, grey, gritty sand and sharp rocks covered the surface. A small mountain loomed not far away. Everything was black, or white, or grey. They had landed on the moon. And the wind was blowing. (And this was strange, as there is no wind on the moon.)

As she looked up, she saw, rising above the mountain in the sky, another ball. This ball was colored - blue with white, green, and brown - a jewel in the dark skies. It looked so beautiful it took her breath away. It was called Earth.

Abblesoc gazed in awe. If only she had landed there. She tried to waken her spacecraft, but all she got was a grunt. The spacecraft slept on, snoring ever so quietly.

As she gazed up at the earth over the mountain, the wind became stronger and seemed to be pushing her towards the mountain. She let the breeze blow her, she stretched out her arms out, and the wind blew her towards the mountain. She started to climb the steep, stony slopes. Once she fell and grazed her knee. She was gasping for breath when, quite suddenly, she came to the top. Her little body was battered and bruised.

The wind died away, and she was left alone, on top of the mountain on the moon.

As she stood there, before her eyes, a moonbeam slowly stretched out before her. But Abblesoc was frightened. The earth looked so far away, floating in the dark sky. The moonbeam shimmered and shone. It seemed to invite her to ride it.

But was it strong enough for her? Did it reach all the way to Earth? What if is stopped half-way and she was left hanging in space?

A gentle shove behind her from the breeze pushed her towards it. She took a big breath, and before she realized what was happening, she was on the moonbeam and shooting down to Earth.

So, she slid, laughing, straight into Tom's warm bed.

Tom was fast asleep. His bed was warm and cozy. Soft covers enclosed her. Tom was dreaming of an alien, just like Abblesoc. Sometimes he made small, twitching movements as he dreamed. But most of the time, he was breathing, in and out, regularly and gently. The cover moved as he breathed, quietly up and down. It was so quiet that Abblesoc could heat Tom's heart beating, slowly as he slept.

He smelled good. Abblesoc felt safe at last. She felt warm and dozy. She knew she could relax.

As she lay in that warm, soft bed, she thought about her long journey. She remembered the tension as they swerved to avoid the stars. She remembered the comets chasing them with their fiery tails. She remembered dodging the stony asteroids that seemed to loom up to fast - and as she remembered them, the memories seemed so far away.

The pictures in her mind grew smaller, the colors faded away, and soon the whole voyage seemed far, far away.

As she lay there in Tom's warm bed, she began to warm up herself. First, her body grew warmer. The tide of warmth crept down her arms to the very tips of her fingers. Then slowly, her little legs grew warmer. Then her feet and, at last, her toes.

Gradually her muscles relaxed. Her body felt heavy and floppy. Her arms and legs felt heavy and floppy. Her eyelids felt heavy...and heavier...and finally closed... Her heart slowed down... Her breathing was gentle - in and out...in and out...

She snuggled up closer. Tom moved over in his sleep, and his breathing caught - and then resumed - in and out... in and out...

As little Abblesoc moved into Tom's dreams, they breathed as one, their hearts beat in time with each other. Gently beating, gently breathing... in and out...her whole body feeling heavier and heavier... her breathing quieter and quieter... in and out...in and out...

Abblesoc the Alien Faces the Bullies

The sun came streaming into the bedroom. It crept down the wall. It moved onto Tom's face.

Tom opened his eyes - yawned and blinked. He stretched - and felt something hard and knobby in his bed. He threw off the cover, and Abblesoc stirred. She was still fast asleep.

Tom gaped at her in astonishment. An alien in HIS bed! Just like the alien in his dreams.

He stroked her; then, he poked her, and Abblesoc opened her eyes.

Her eyes were silver, not blue, not brown, not green, not even grey - but a bright, shiny silver Her thick wavy hair was silver, too. Not brown, not yellow, not black, not even grey - but a bright, shiny silver. She was wearing her green space suit - and she still had her boots on - in bed!

"Who are you?" asked Tom. "And what are you doing in my bed?"

Now Abblesoc had many gifts - and one was that she could understand any Earth language - and more besides. But she didn't know what to say.

Now Tom was a practical little boy. (He was only five years old and not much bigger than Abblesoc.) It was breakfast time, and Tom was hungry. He climbed out of bed and pulled Abblesoc out, too. He held tightly to her hand and pulled her along the landing, down the stairs to the kitchen.

Abblesoc wasn't afraid of Tom. He seemed friendly and not too big. But in the kitchen was a HUGE, GINORMOUS Earth person. Abblesoc was terrified. Tom's mom was astonished - what had Tom been up to now!

"I found it in my bed," explained Tom.

"In your bed?" repeated his mom.

"Yes, and she had her boots on - in bed."

"Had her boots on?" said his mom.

"Mommmmm," said Tom. "And we are both hungry."

Tom set Abblesoc down at the breakfast table and poured out some "Alien Monster Flakes" cereal into both dishes. Then he poured out some milk without spilling too much on the table. Abblesoc watched to see what she should do.

"Eat," said Tom. So, she ate - and ate - and ate. More cereal was added to her bowl, more milk was poured over it - and still, Abblesoc ate. She had never had anything so delicious. Even Tom was amazed at how much the little alien could eat. Her tummy seemed to be getting bigger - and bigger.

"Perhaps she'll explode?" thought Tom.

Now Abblesoc just wanted to go back to the nice, warm bed and sleep for a week, But Tom had other ideas! And he was a determined little boy. He wanted to show Abblesoc to his friends. He pulled her to the door, but Abblesoc sat down on the floor and refused to budge.

Tom didn't know what to do.

"I'll let you ride on my new bicycle," he said. "It's got training wheels, so you won't fall off."

Abblesoc wasn't interested. She had ridden thousands and thousands of miles in a spaceship.

So, Tom had to go off to play by himself.

He told his friends about Abblesoc – and they didn't believe him. (Would you have believed him?)

He told the postman about Abblesoc – and he didn't believe Tom, either.

He even told the cat about Abblesoc – and the cat just walked away with her tail in the air.

No one believed him. Tom felt cross and disappointed. He went back in and told his mommy.

"No one believes me," he said sadly.

His mommy had gotten over her amazement. They went up and looked at the little alien lying in Tom's bed, but Abblesoc wasn't asleep. She felt a bit mean not going out with Tom, who had been so kind to her.

"Why don't you want to go out and play?" asked Tom's mommy.

"I'm so frightened of getting lost and not being able to find my way back." Said the little alien.

"We need three things to make you safe," said mommy.

"First – know where we live. Number 3, Greenacre Road, Whizzytown."

"Planet Earth," added Tom.

"Second – what looks special about our house?"

"We have a blue front door," said Tom, "and yellow curtains at the windows."

"Third – you need to go out and explore with Tom. He will look after you and show you where we live."

But first, mommy went out into the street and took a color photograph of their house. She gave it to Abblesoc. "This will help you recognize our home," she said.

So, Tom took Abblesoc out to explore and teach her the way home. He was riding his new bicycle – Abbelsoc had decided she would rather walk. They went a short way along the road.

A group of bigger boys were feeling bored and decided to borrow Tom's bicycle. Tom didn't want to let them have it. He was afraid they would damage it. But he was frightened of the bigger boys. His legs were trembling, and his mouth felt dry. They started to argue, and the big boys were getting nasty. They hadn't noticed Abblesoc, who was very small.

But Abblesoc had noticed them. She jumped in front of Tom and told them they were bullies and to leave Tom alone. The boys were so surprised that such a tiny person would dare to tell them off that they slouched off, grumbling. Then, after a few steps, they realized that that tiny person looked different – sharp, fiery silver eyes and strange silver hair.

Tom rode home as fast as he could. Abblesoc hitched a lift on the back of his bicycle. The boys watched them go – thinking, "What was that?"

Tom thought Abblesoc was very brave. She was so small – yet, she had faced the bullies, and they had turned away.

Tom was riding so fast he went right through a rather large puddle of murky water. Abblesoc got drenched. She loved it! "Do that again!" she begged Tom.

So, they played in the muddy puddle for a while. They were both getting wetter and dirtier and dirtier and wetter by the minute. All too soon, Tom heard his mom calling – time to go home!

When the two appeared at the door, Tom's mom knew exactly what to do.

"Upstairs," she said. "Bath time!"

Tom and Abblesoc looked at each other. Bath time again? But they knew it would be nice to get clean.

So, Tom's mom ran a bath. The water was warm. The soapy water tasted - well - it tasted of soap! They made little waves and watched the water slopping over the edge of the bathtub; then they thought they should stop. They didn't want to make the floor all wet.

They blew bubbles in the water and watched them floating up to the ceiling. They tried to count the colors on the bubbles, but there were too many. Sometimes one of the bubbles would go sailing out of the window. They tried to make the biggest bubbles they could - taking deep, deep breaths and then a long, slow blow.

They lay down in the warm water and enjoyed the feeling, as it seemed to stroke their skin. Abblesoc had never felt like this - ever.

Blowing the bubbles in the warm water, the two friends were almost sorry when mommy came in with two big fluffy towels. The brown water drained away, making that gurgly sound as it went down the drain.

Warm as toast and squeaky clean, the two friends sat down to tea. Abblesoc had faced the bullies, and Tom had found a new friend.

Abblesoc goes to the farm - and learns we are all different and valued

Abblesoc and Tom were going to visit the farm. It was a fine sunny day, with a keen wind blowing. It rustled Abblesoc's hair, and it blew the hat off Tom's mom's head. Tom and Abblesoc went running after it. Who would catch it? Who could catch it?

The hat blew up high in the air, and Tom jumped as high as he could. He made a grab - but he missed.

The hat flew on and landed in a tree - too high for Tom's mom to reach.

Abblesoc said, "I'm light and strong - I could climb the tree and get your hat."

So Abblesoc climbed up the tree and reached the hat. She gripped it between her teeth so that she could use her hands to climb back down. Tom's mom was pleased to have her hat back - even though it had a big bite on the side. She tied it back on with a scarf. It wouldn't blow off now.

They reached the gate leading into the farmyard. Farmer Giles came over to greet them. With the farmer came Gruff, the black and white sheepdog.

Now, Abblesoc the alien had one gift that neither Tom nor his mom had. She could understand what the animals were saying. So Abblesoc asked Gruff what use he was - she wasn't very polite - but Gruff was a kind dog, and he simply wagged his tail and said, "My job is to round up the sheep for the farmer. It's a very important job. I guide the sheep into safe places - no one else could do my job."

Abblesoc wasn't impressed.

"I could do that, it's easy," she said.

Famer Giles asked her what was easy, so she told him.

"Well, you could try. I need six sheep from the field to be put into the pen here. Go on; you get them. (If you can.)" he thought, smiling to himself.

So Abblesoc ran into the field and started to try to get the sheep into the pen. The sheep just looked at her and carried on chewing. Abelson shouted at them - and soon, they all ran away to the far side of the field. Gruff ran after Abblesoc and said, "You mustn't frighten the sheep - it's not kind."

"But, the silly sheep won't do as they are told."

"Watch me," said Gruff.

He very quietly sank down and slid along the field to one side of the sheep. You could hardly see him move. Then farmer Giles whistled, and Gruff surged to his feet. He nudged the sheep towards the pen. He wasn't rough, but he was firm. Most of the sheep went straight into the pen. But there is always one - isn't there?

This sheep decided to run the wrong way. Gruff wasn't having that. He chased after with all his speed - far faster than Abblesoc could run - and chased the sheep into the pen in no time at all. The sheep were safe in pen. Gruff wasn't even out of breath, and farmer Giles was pleased.

"Thank you, Gruff," he said, "I don't know what I would do without you."

Just then, Farmer Giles's son, Harry, came over. He was going to take them round to meet the other animals.

"First, let's go into the yard and meet the chickens," said Harry.

The little brown chickens were running about freely. They looked so cute.

"May I pick one up?" asked Abblesoc. Harry showed her how to pick up the chicken gently without hurting it. She stroked the soft downy feathers and noticed all he many colors as the sun glinted among the feathers; brown - but also gold and red and deeper brown. Abblesoc took a deep breath - and sneezed.

The chicken flew down, and Abblesoc asked her whether she did anything useful.

"Yes," said the chicken, "I lay eggs for the farmer's breakfast, fresh, every day."

"Have you laid any eggs today?" asked Harry.

The chicken clucked, and Harry followed her into the henhouse; there, the chicken proudly showed Harry two new-laid eggs, one for Tom and one for Abblesoc!

Abblesoc thanked the chicken. The chicken could do something she couldn't do. She couldn't lay and eggs for breakfast, and neither could Tom!

Harry took them into the pasture. It was a bit muddy, and the mud was sticky. It made walking a little bit difficult, lifting her shoes out of the mud every squelchy step. They saw the cows, and the cows saw them.

Abblesoc wondered where Gruff was. "We don't bring a dog into a field of cows," said Harry. " The cows don't like it, and they can run faster than people, and you might get hurt."

The cows seemed gentle with their beautiful big brown eyes and soft-looking brown hair.

"Can I stroke the cow?" asked Abblesoc.

"Yes, if you are very gentle. They like to be stroked. Abblesoc reached up and stroked the soft hair; so did Tom. The cows breathed with great sighing sounds, their breath warm smelling nicely of a cow. One cow mooed softly in the distance.

"You must never go in a field where the cow has babies, though," said Harry. "They might think you are a danger to their baby and attack you."

He showed them another small field where there was a cow with her calf. The calf looked so sweet with its long, unsteady legs, drinking from its mommy.

"Cows give us milk, and we make cheese and butter and yogurt from the milk," said Harry. "Cows are very useful animals, so we look after them carefully."

"I like cows," said Abblesoc.

"So do I," said Tom. "I like the milk for my cereal in the morning, too."

"Now, I have something very special for you to see," said Harry. He took them to a far corner of the field where there was a small pond.

"What can you see?" asked Harry. He wasn't going to tell them.

Abblesoc and Tom gazed around. They saw a weeping willow tree, its drooping branches looking at itself on the water. They saw some reeds around the edge. They looked up and saw birds sitting on the branches of the tree high up. They looked higher and saw fluffy white clouds sailing by overhead.

Suddenly Tom slapped his arm. "I've been bitten," he cried. A small gnat had, indeed, bitten him. But it was only a small bite, and soon it stopped itching. Still, he wanted no more bites.

"Look down in the water," said Harry.

They looked.

"Ugh," said Abblesoc. "Slimy, jelly-like stuff with black dots in it, ugh."

Then she saw a green frog sitting on a stone near the center of the pond, watching her with its red, bulging eyes. It flicked out an enormously long tongue, catching and swallowing a fly.

"Oh," cried Abblesoc. "Did you see that, Tom? The frog eats the flies, so you won't get bitten. Another very useful animal!"

Harry told them that the jelly-like slimy stuff with the black dots was the frog's eggs, just waiting to hatch into tadpoles and them to grow arms and strong legs and long sticky tongues to become frogs.

Harry took Abblesoc and Tom back to the farm, where Tom's mom was sitting happily in the kitchen, chatting to farmer Giles's wife. They had a drink of milk, and then it was time to go home.

Abblesoc and Tom waved goodbye to the cows in the meadow. They said goodbye to the chickens in the yard. Gruff came to wave, then off wagging his tail.

That night Abbelsoc tried to remember all the animals she had met. The clever dog Gruff, who could race so fast, yet could also be gentle and patient. The chickens - so soft to stroke. The cows with their big, brown eyes and the frog, with the baby eggs, are just waiting to become grown-up frogs and catch flies.

Every animal had its place. Every animal has its own gifts. Every animal was different, just as she was. Every animal has its own talents - and so did she. It was OK to be different. It was good to be oneself, special and unique...

She imagined stroking the chickens soft, soft feathers. So soft... She felt the soft hairs of the gentle cows again... She felt the sighing breath of the cow again... and breathed in its nice cow smell... She imagined the low moo...such a sleepy sound...soon her eyes closed... soon she drifted off... back to the farm...with Gruff...and the chickens...and the cows...and lots of tiny baby frogs...too many to count...

Abblesoc Meets Dr. Bob

One fine morning, Tom's mom gave Tom and Abblesoc a paper bag. She told them there was a surprise inside. She asked them to find a nice place to stop awhile before they looked inside.

So Abblesoc and Tom went to look for a nice tree - one tall enough so they had a good view and one that had plenty of places where they could sit and find out what was in the bag.

The first tree Tom found was too prickly. That wouldn't be comfortable!

Then Abblesoc found a tall tree - but there was no place to sit down on it.

At last, they did find a tree at the bottom of the field. This tree was tall, but it had lots of wide branches they could sit on. They climbed up - and up - and up. They settled themselves in a high place where two big branches forked. And then they looked inside the paper bag.

"Plums," said Tom. "I love plums."

Abblesoc had never seen plums before. "What do you do with plums?" she asked.

"This," said Tom - and he ate one. It was big and juicy; it tasted sweet - but also a little bit sour.

Abblesoc took a bite - and tasted the sweet, juicy plum. She pulled a face - it's a bit sour," she said.

"Have another," said Tom.

And she did.

After a while, as they sat in the tall tree, eating the plums, Abblesoc felt her tummy was feeling a bit full. But she liked the plums and ate another - and another. Her tummy was feeling funny - not a very happy feeling. Tom was still tucking into the plums. Abblesoc took another - it was the last one.

Soon her tummy felt most uncomfortable! "Let's go back to the house now," she said.

Tom didn't want to leave the high tree just yet - he felt full and comfortable. His tummy didn't hurt. But Abblesoc was looking funny. She was not her delicate shade of blue - but green, a weird, dark green. Tom began to get worried.

He climbed down the tree. Climbing down isn't as easy as climbing up; soon, he was stuck. He didn't know whether to put his left foot down or to hang on with his hands and hope his right foot would find a branch to step down on. His foot began to shake.

He managed to scramble down, scraping his knee and banging his shoulder on the way. Abblesoc slid down, bedside him. Tree climbing was easier for her. She had strong little arms, and she as much lighter than Tom. But her tummy was hurting. She bent over, holding her tummy with both hands.

They staggered back to the house. Mommy was very upset to see them looking so miserable. She hadn't meant them to eat ALL the plums, and she didn't know that plums would disagree with Abblesoc. Abblesoc was an alien, and there were many things Tom's mom didn't know about her.

She decided to take Abblesoc to see Dr. Tom. She thought a check-up would be a good idea.

Dr. Bob was an old-fashioned country doctor.

He was wise, he was friendly, and he knew nearly everyone. And nearly everyone liked Dr. Bob.

But Abblesoc had other ideas.

"I'm perfectly well," she had said, looking green. "I don't want to see the doctor," she insisted. "I won't go," she had shouted, stamping her little foot.

Tom said, "He's got a nice fluffy cat called Fudge."

"I don't care," said Abblesoc. "I won't go."

"But Fudge would like you to stroke him," said Tom, very quietly. "He's got the loudest purr."

Now Abblesoc did like cats, even though to her they were enormous, as big as a tiger would seem to you or me.

"He's got blue eyes – like me," said Tom. He could see that Abblesoc was weakening. And her tummy was very sore.

"But Dr. Tom only lets good children stroke him; perhaps you are not good enough." Tom sounded sad, although inside he was grinning.

"I am good," said Abblesoc. "I will stroke Fudge."

Tom's mom hurried them out of the door before Abblesoc changed her mind.

They reached the doctor's office, and there was Dr. Tom waiting for them with a big smile. Tom's mom had told him a little bit about Abblesoc on the phone.

"Come on into my room," said Dr. Tom, "Fudge as been waiting to meet you, Abblesoc."

He didn't sound scary, so Abblesoc went into the doctor's office - and there was the biggest, fluffiest cat she had ever seen. Abblesoc was enchanted. She went up to Fudge and started to stroke him.

"I can see you are a very brave girl," said Dr. Tom. "I have some things to show you, too."

Abblesoc smiled - this was fun.

Dr. Bob asked her to open her mouth so he could tickle her tonsils.

"Say ahhhh," he said, and Abblesoc said, "ahhhh."

"What are tonsils?" asked Abbelsoc.

Dr. Bob asked Tom to show Abblesoc his tonsils. "Right there at the back of his throat are two little reddish lumps. Those are his tonsils," said Dr. Bob. "But you don't seem to have any - so I can't tickle them!"

"Can I tickle Tom's?" asked Abblesoc. Her tummy was beginning to feel less sore.

"Better not," replied the doctor. "I once knew a little boy who tried to tickle his tonsils with a fork - and swallowed it. Not a good idea."

All this time, Dr. Tom was looking at Abblesoc.

"What a strange color," he thought. "Is she always green?"

"Here's my special doctor's torch," he said. "May I look in your ears with it?"

Abblesoc kept very still while Dr. Bob looked in her ears. They were blue inside, with tiny hairs, and a dark blue circle at the back.

"Hmmm - they look good," he said. "Now, look in my ears if you want."

Abblesoc took the torch and very gently looked in Dr. Bob's ears. "I can't see much," she said.

Dr. Bob reached for his stethoscope. "Well," he said. You will be able to hear something if you listen carefully, but it's my turn first."

He placed the end of the stethoscope on her chest and asked Tom to take Fudge out of the room. He was purring so loudly that Dr. Bob couldn't hear properly. He listened, and he heard not the soft be-boom, be-boom of a child's heart but a tick, tick, tick, tick sound – just like clockwork.

"Well," he said, "you've got a good little ticker in there." And he let Abblesoc listen. And then Tom came back, and he had a listen, too, before letting Fudge back in.

Finally, Dr. Bob looked at Abblesoc's tummy.

"Where does it hurt?" he asked.

Abblesoc thought for a moment. Her tummy had stopped hurting; her color was returning to its normal shade of blue. She had the palest blue skin – as smooth as concrete.

"Well," said Dr. Bob. "I think you ate too many plums – but you will be fine now. Just don't be so greedy next time!" he added with a smile and a twinkle in his eye.

Abblesoc, Tom, and Tom's mom went home.

"I think you need a rest, Abblesoc," said Tom's mom. "Settle down on the settee. Tom and I will make sandwiches for tea while you have a little sleep."

So Abblesoc settled down for a rest. She didn't feel sleepy – but it did feel good not to have a sore tummy. She felt it under her hands, soft and warm. She stretched out. She thought about what had happened and decide that she needed to listen to her body. If her tummy told her it was full, she should stop eating.

As she lay, half asleep, she was thinking about what a wonderful thing her body was. It was different from Tom's, but it was hers- and she knew that she would be aware of it. If it seemed uncomfortable, she would notice and stop hurting it. She stretched again... And relaxed.

The sun shone into the room and warmed her. She heard the sounds of Tom and his mom in the kitchen; they were faint, but she liked to hear them. They made her feel safe.

She relaxed all her muscles - first her toes and then her legs. She let the feeling of warmth and softness spread up her body... her back... and her front. She nestled her head on the cushion and let her neck relax... Her face relaxed... her mouth half-open... she closed her eyes... Her eyelids relaxed... she felt so warm and soft. She lay quiet and content as the sunbeams moved across the room...

Abblesoc and the Snowman

Abblesoc opened her eyes. It was morning, and Tom was still sound asleep. But it seemed very quiet. Somehow the air seemed muffled.

The little alien got quietly out of bed and went to the window. She drew the curtain and... she saw a grey sky. It was full of white flakes floating and falling through the air. Abblesoc opened the window and leaned out to have a better look. The lawn beneath was white, not green. The trees were coated with white - and it was cold. Very cold.

Tom stirred. "Shut the window. It's freezing," he mumbled.

Abblesoc leaned out and caught some falling snowflakes; they were cold. She ran across the room and stuffed them down Tom's neck.

Tom yelped and sat up angrily.

Tom saw the open window - he saw the snow, falling, falling.

Tom catapulted, put of bed, and ran to the window. "It's snowing, it's snowing, it's snowing!" he cried.

Tom and Abblesoc got dressed in no time at all and rushed downstairs. They were just pulling on their boots when Tom's mom appeared.

"Breakfast first," she said firmly. She made them sit down and eat some toast to keep them warm. Then she pulled out a drawer and took out a bobble hat for Tom - it was red. Then she rummaged some more and found another bobble hat for Abblesoc - it was green.

"I'm not putting on that funny hat," said Abblesoc.

"That's fine then; you won't be going out either - no hat, no snow!"

Abblesoc put on the funny hat, and Tom tried not to giggle – she did look rather funny! But so did he.

They put on their boots and scarves, coats, and gloves. Then they dashed outside.

Abblesoc stood and stared. She had never seen snow before. It smelled strange – a sort of tangy smell. While she was standing still, Tom scooped up a handful of snow and ran towards her – but she saw him coming and dodged away. Soon they were throwing snowballs at each other, shouting and laughing. They felt as warm as the toast they had had for breakfast.

A friend of Tom's came running over –"Can I play?" he asked. For the answer, Tom threw a snowball at him – but missed. Soon, several children were playing on Tom's front lawn. They were gathering up the snow and throwing it, catching it, even someone's little dog joined in the fun. The little dog was clever at catching the snowballs, but he pulled such a funny face as the cold snow went into his mouth. He didn't know whether to eat it or spit it out.

The children skidded and slid in the snow. They ran, slid, and laughed. They were out of breath; they were happy.

Tom showed Abblesoc how to make an angel in the snow – Abblesoc had never seen an angel. Neither had Tom, but he knew how to lie down in the snow and wave his arms up and down to make the wings. His coat was getting wetter and wetter, but Tom was warm and his hand warm and tingly inside his gloves.

The children decided to make a snowman. The bigger kids rolled a small snowball along the side of the lawn. As they rolled, the snowball got bigger and bigger and bigger. Then with a big heave, they turned it up, and the snowman's body was set in the center of the lawn.

Meanwhile, Abblesoc, Tom, and some of the smaller kids were rolling another snowball for the head. One of the biggest boys picked it up and set it on the snowman's body. "It doesn't look much like a man," thought Abblesoc.

"We need a hat and scarf," cried one boy.

"And a carrot for the nose," cried another.

"I'll find some stones for the buttons," said a very small boy.

Tom went indoors to ask his mom for a spare scarf and hat - and a carrot. He took them outside. He stuck in the nose and plonked the hat on top of the snowman's head. The snowman was beginning to look like a snowman - but he needed eyes and a mouth. Abblesoc found a twig, which made him a smiley mouth, and the little kid had scrabbled around and found three pebbles for buttons.

"What shall we use for eyes?" they asked each other.

Abblesoc thought for a moment. She went inside and asked, very politely, if Tom's mom had two big, black buttons they could use. Tom's mom looked inside her sewing box - and sure enough, there were two big, black buttons. She gave them to Abblesoc. Abblesoc ran outside and placed the buttons carefully in the snowman's face. They all stood back to admire him - he looked perfect.

The kids decided to have one last snowball fight before. It was time to go to their homes for dinner. And as always seems to happen, the last snowballs of the day sailed straight through Tom's front window.

The glass cracked and shattered. The kids ran and scattered. Tom and Abblesoc went inside to see the damage.

Tom's mom was a little bit cross - the broken window would have to be repaired. But really, it was quite funny, wasn't it? She wasn't cross for long. The kids had had such fun in the snow - and there was big snowman on the front lawn.

She helped Tom and Abblesoc get their boots off - and their wet scarves, and wet hats, and wet gloves, and wet coats. They both felt tired and a bit sleepy. They relaxed in the warm room and ate their supper at the kitchen table. Soon it was time to go up the wooden hills to bed.

Tom's dad read them a story, as he did every night. A special time for him with Tom and Abblesoc. Tom drifted off to sleep, and soon he was dreaming of snowmen and buttons and carrots and...

Abblesoc was sleepy, but she wanted to see the snowman again. She walked over to the window and drew back the curtain. There he was, standing in the middle of the lawn, just as they had left him.

She wondered if he was cold out there in the dark. But then she thought that he looked happy and peaceful in his cold, white world. She thought she saw him wink at her.

She went back to bed, feeling content. She had helped to make a snowman! She had made some new friends. Together, they had made something special. She snuggled down under the covers.

Abblesoc stretched out and wriggled her toes... She relaxed her toes...She wriggled her legs... and relaxed her legs. She wriggled her arms... and relaxed her arms... She wriggled her neck and body...and relaxed her whole body. She gave a great sigh and fell fast asleep.

www.ingramcontent.com/pod-product-compliance
Lightning Source LLC
Chambersburg PA
CBHW070049230426
43661CB00005B/822